# THE ADVENTURES
## *of*
# *Moochie*

*Steven "Moochie" Knowles*

ISBN 978-1-64349-878-2 (paperback)
ISBN 978-1-64349-879-9 (digital)

Christian Faith Publishing, Inc.
832 Park Avenue
Meadville, PA 16335
www.christianfaithpublishing.com

Printed in the United States of America

This is the story of growing up in a small Midwestern town in the heart of America. The small town is Goddard, Kansas, and if you look at a map of the United States of America, point to the center and you will find it! At the time of my growing up, it was 12 miles west of Wichita, Kansas. It is the story of Moochie and what that growing up was like in that town of less than 150 people.

*The Adventures of Moochie* is a collection of short stories that tell some of the adventures of Moochie. Each short story tells of a different adventure or at least a different event in Moochie's life. Each is true, or at least as true as Moochie can remember. In some there is collaboration with others. With brothers Jim, Chuck, Bill, and Bob it is in "The Vagabond Family," "The Box of Everything," and smaller roles in other stories. Mike Teter (class of 1967) has his additions in the "Mike and Moochie" story. Phil Wohlford's in the "Phil and his Scribe, Moochie" story. I must also thank Mike Herndon (1967) for being the inspiration in "The Empty Chair." Of course, Dr. Richard Steckley (class of, what else, 1967) has to be included, as without his and his staffs efforts, *The Adventures of Moochie* would never have been completed. Susan Shaw, class of, what else, 1967, brought her editing talents and writing talents to the group performing what nobody else could. After twenty plus years at Wichita Eagle, needless to say she was very good at her job! With Susan joining the group, it basically became a class, family, and friends project!

Susan also added her recollection of her favorite "Moochie" story of being in seventh grade when one of our teachers noted that all of my classmates called me "Moochie." The teacher asked the class, "Why does everyone call Steven, Moochie? Is he always mooching pencils or notebook paper?" The class LOUDLY responded with "BECAUSE he looks just like Moochie on TV!"

My sons, John and Marc, also added not only the making of the numerous copies for everyone to read and evaluate each story but also their talents in "fleshing out" the stories.

The people in the stories are real people; their names have not been changed to protect the innocent. They were more than just people; they were my friends! Heck, we were all just kids! Even as we grew older, in Moochie's mind, they were always just the scruffy little boys and girls that inhabited Moochie's world.

The stories oftentimes overlap other adventures as time and events that happen in *The Adventures of Moochie* are fluid in nature and often happen at the same time as other adventures. Got it!

This goes back to all the roles that we play in life. We are many different people to those around us. To my children, John and Marc, I am their Dad. To Dathan, Delica, Hevin, John Jr., Troy, Sterling, and Mary, I am Grandpa, or Papa. To my brothers, Jim, Chuck, Bill, and Bob, I am their brother. To my friends, I am a friend, and hopefully a true friend! It is how we relate to others that makes us unique! So how many stories that we have in us is only limited by our life span! Got that, So far!

So here are *The Adventures of Moochie*! I hope everyone enjoys my retelling of them as I lived them or maybe I should say as Moochie lived them! It is written "In Moochie," so we should start with learning the rules of Moochie-isms.

The stories come from the head and the memories it holds there. The poems come from a heart that had to experience what inspired them. Now both stories and poems are parts of me and my life. One poem, not mine, but a song that I cherish in my heart and mind (all songs start out as poems), is *My Way* by Paul Anka. (mr) . . . (Moochie rules for run-on sentences). This song seems to say it all!

## "My Way"

And now the end is near
So I face the final curtain
My friend, I'll say it clear
I'll state my case of which I'm certain
I've lived a life that's full
I've traveled each and every highway
And more, much more than this
I did it my way

Regrets I've had a few
But then again, too few to mention
I did what I had to do
And saw through without exemption
I planned each charted course
Each careful step along the byway
Oh, and more, much more than this
I did it my way

Yes, there were times,
I'm sure you knew
When I bit off more than I could chew
But through it all when there was doubts
I ate it up and spit it out
I faced it all and I stood tall
And did it my way

I've loved, I've laughed and cried
I've had my fill, my share of losing
And now as tears subside
I find it all so amusing
To think I did all that
And may I say, not in a shy way
Oh, no, no not me
I did it my way

For what is a man, what has he got
If not himself, then he has not
To say all the things he truly feels
And not the words of one who kneels
The record shows I took the blows
And did it my way

Paul Anka wrote it for Frank Sinatra. But many others including Elvis Presley and nearly every other artist that could carry a tune, including the writer Paul Anka, performed a version of this song.

# *Talking or Thinking in Moochie*

I decided from comments made by readers of my stuff that I needed to lay the ground rules of Moochie-isms. I have realized that I don't speak, think, or write in English! I talk, I write, and I think in Moochie. I'll try to explain; Maynard G. Krebs (Bob Denver in *The Many Loves of Dobie Gillis*) spoke in "beatnik," and most people developed an understanding of what he was talking about. In his next role as Gilligan in *Gilligan's Isle*, he did not speak "beatnik," but he kind of kept the likeable personality style of Maynard G. Krebs Well, "talking in Moochie" is somewhat like that. While "thinking in Moochie" may be more complex, it may become a little easier to interpret or translate to others if those that translate had some of the thought process of Moochie to understand Moochie. GOT THAT, so far?

How did Moochie become Moochie? First of all, my real name is Steve. When my family moved to the small Midwestern town of Goddard, Kansas, I was in the second grade. Now we may have only had about twenty kids in second grade, but two of those were named Steve. Our first teacher decided that only one would be called Steve and the other, Steven. I was the other! This worked for about a day; we became confused (I was only six; the first Steve was seven), and the teacher also became a little confused, as she started to just point at one of the Steves when she ask something of the Steves. She then decided to use our last name's first letter as a way to separate the Steves. Are you confused yet? Well, both Steve and Steven were, as well as the teacher!

I don't remember how long this went on, but the first Steve, him, not the other Steve, me, came up with the answer! The first Steve had watched *Spin and Marty* and *The Mickey Mouse Club* a lot. He noticed a child actor named Kevin Corcoran whose character in both shows was named Moochie, and he was almost a twin of the "other" Steve, me! So I, Moochie, was born! This reminds me of a skit on *Laugh-In* where Arte Johnson and Peter Sellers were playing the two Nazis behind the bush. Arte Johnson said, "We look alike; I can't tell us apart," to which Peter Sellers said, "You are the other one!" I was the other one, and I am Moochie!

This use of *Laugh-In* out of nowhere is the first example of "thinking in Moochie." Moochie is allowed to, at any time, bring in any movie, any character, any TV show, in fact anything, if it can be tied into the subject or story in any way! This is Rule Number One! Movies and TV were not the only things that ran constantly in Moochie's head. "Rock and roll" songs would later also enter Moochie's brain, and if Moochie was in a "rock and roll" mood, the lyrics would become what Moochie shared and used in "Moochie-isms." Can anybody hear the lines, "A candy colored clown they call the sandman . . . Tiptoes to my room every night . . . Just to sprinkle star dust and to whisper . . . Go to sleep everything is all right . . . I close my eyes and drift away." And not hear Roy Orbison? Is there anyone that doesn't hear my favorite song after that . . . going through their head? The trick is how do you get it out of your head? By the way, the song is *In Dreams* by Roy Orbison, DUH!

Any sentence used to explain this added thought can run as long as Moochie can continue the connection in any way. This is Rule Number Two! Example one of Rule Number Two: remember Gracie Allen during her monologues with George Burns; Gracie could make a sentence last for an entire paragraph (mr). I have a granddaughter named Mary who I call "the Gracie Two" because, although I can't understand a word she says (she is only 19 months), she rattles on as if I could! This is the basis behind Rule Number Two! And is noted by the (mr) indicating a run-on sentence being used (Moochie rules). Another aspect of this could be the affect, not only to the translation but also how a story can expand on its own! George Burns would stop Gracie's rambling with "Say Goodnight, Gracie." To wit Gracie replied, "Goodnight, Gracie!" Example two of rule two: later on, *Laugh-In* would end with Dan saying, "Say Goodnight, Dick." To wit Dick would reply, "Goodnight, Dick," as would many of the cast and guests who would also follow with them saying, "Goodnight, Dick!" Anybody notice the tie-in of the stories?

In translating Moochie, one also has to be on the lookout for certain keywords or phrases like oops. The "oops" usually means that a change in thought or position is coming or has already come! Sometimes it is a total reversal, a

180 degree, or a clarification meant to reverse any pain that might have been caused by the first position. The "oops" is Rule Number Three! Another guide to Rule Three is when Moochie starts degrading Moochie . . . This usually means that an earlier Moochie position has been proven wrong and the second Moochie has to declare the first Moochie as the loser. (mr) This is kind of like the character "Eve" that Joanne Woodward played in *The Three Faces of Eve*, a study on split personality. The second Moochie takes the opposite view of whatever subject and degrades the first Moochie for expressing that earlier position. In *The Three Faces of Eve*, it would be "Eve Black" degrading "Eve White" for all who stay up late watching old movies. Classic split personality syndrome! If the first Moochie got into a fight with the second Moochie, who would win? Answer, always the OTHER one!

Rule Number Four deals with words left out in sentences leaving the reader with what is known as "gibberish." Many of these are small insignificant words because of "Moochie's" mind-racing problem. Another isn't caused by a racing mind, but instead it is caused by Moochie's terrible spelling ability, as one of our grade school teachers (Mr. Porter) noted on Moochie's grade card to my Mom, "Steve (for some reason he always called me that) is doing well, but he really needs to work on his spelling!" (mr, of course) Another thing Moochie has to contend with: blind spots in his vision. A fourth problem is taking the *not* or *n't* and leaving it off of where it should go. This often causes a 180-degree swing in the meaning being given to the reader. Or it could be Moochie just "covering his bases" as it allows

Moochie to claim his position is correct no matter which side is proven correct "or not" covering both sides even if Moochie does not actually put it there (got to be mr). GOT that, so far? I guess, "oops" should be inserted somewhere, but sometimes Moochie doesn't even see it. Those blind spots again cause Moochie to actually believe he has put a correct thought or sentence together, but all of the words may not be there to make it readable. (mr) It often takes a well-versed translator in "thinking Moochie" to make "heads or tails" out of Moochie "speaking Moochie." I think there were only three who were well versed in understanding "Moochie speak": Herndon, Hansen, and Steeby; sounds like a law firm, doesn't it. Only the one who caused it to exist is still with us, the first "Steve" . . . Steeby.

Those are the four main rules of understanding how "Moochie think, speak, and write." But there are others that a person has to understand in order to understand "Moochie." One is "third person thought." This is the ability for "Moochie" to go outside of "Moochie" and talk about "Moochie" as another person. GOT THAT! So far!

This has allowed me (Moochie) to take risks because I could convince myself that it was not me who was risking injury or death but "Moochie!" Strange, huh; weird huh! It is funny how the mind can be trained to accept almost anything! It is weird, but I bet many people go into "third person" to accept the danger of their actions. This might be how a soldier deals with his, and now her, actions in war. Going against the natural basic need to survive, a soldier may be able to go into "third person" in dangerous situations and convince himself, or herself, that he, or she will survive and tomorrow he, or she, will laugh at being scared of the so-called risk. (mr) See the next paragraph below on "time travel" which is also a part of Moochie talking Moochie!

Another is the ability to "time travel" with language. Yes, there are tenses in language: past, present, and future. But Moochie can use them in other ways. Just the phrase "in a hundred years it will not matter what happens today" is a foil for Moochie to hide in . . . and sometimes to accept a stupid stunt that he did! It could have been a statement Moochie made, and only after it was out of his mouth, he would realize the effect it had made on others. Or it could be the effect that Moochie thought it MIGHT make on others! Or it might have been silence where it should have been talk. But in Moochie's world it has to be covered by the "in a hundred years it will not matter" being inserted!

Now writing in Moochie has some strange habits like all of a sudden you might find a word CAPITALIZED for no apparent reason in the middle of a sentence. That is Moochie SHOUTING the words to put even more emphasis or more importance to the word or WORDS! IT IS ALSO Moochie saying to not only read the sentence BUT think about the MEANING of it. Sometimes Moochie uses the words HELLO or DUH in the same way. Moochie also uses three periods . . . to put a pause in to not only pause it but to express Moochie's feeling about what is being said. It maybe dissatisfaction or just a point of separation! (mr) Moochie also uses the addition of exclamation marks along the same lines! Like THINK ABOUT IT! GOT THAT! SO far! Or SO FAR!

Language will always be a fun way to communicate thoughts and ideas; I hope everyone will now know the nuances of "Moochie speak, write, and think." But always remember "in a hundred years it will not matter!" Nor will the character of "Moochie" even exist, but in a scene from *Old Yeller* where "Moochie's" (Kevin's not Steve's) dog, "Old Yeller," dies! Actually Tommie Kirk (remember Tommie Kirk) had to shoot "Old Yeller" because "Old Yeller" got rabies and threatened Moochie's character. GOT THAT, So Far! . . . That scene may still exist somewhere in the vault of old movies saved by someone! But because the kid character in *Old Yeller* or in *Toby Tyler* was not called Moochie, maybe Kevin Corcoran will come out from that "Moochie" character's shadow and be known as KEVIN CORCORAN! By the way, Moochie's dog (mine, not Moochie's, Kevin's) was Sandy! Confused yet? I know I am.

The child actor, Kevin Corcoran, who played "Moochie" in those *Walt Disney* films, was just like me, in more ways than looks. He could never again be thought of by his real name; he was "Moochie" in films. Whatever role he played, he was known by the "Moochie" role he played as a kid. I became the "Moochie" of Goddard, Kansas, fame! I also found I could never shake it either, so I've finally embraced and accepted it! Kind of like the expression "if you can't beat 'em, then join them!"

I hope Kevin Corcoran was able to remember the "Moochie" role fondly before he passed away. Not seeing it as the albatross that he had to carry all of his life, like many actors who get typecast as a certain character. The main actors in the *Adventures of Superman* could never take another role and be believed in that role of another character. In fact George Reeves (Superman) may have committed suicide because of what it did to his career. It took Sean Connery years to get out of the shadow of "James Bond."

I don't believe that Kevin Corcoran ever really played "Moochie," he just played himself, and it has been said that Walt Disney personally came up with the name for the character. Kevin's portrayal was kind of like what "William Wallace" (Mel Gibson) told one of his captains, "Steven," in "Braveheart," when "Steven" said, "I don't know how to act among all of these fine people." Mel Gibson's character replied to Steven, "Just be yourself!" (mr) Well I believe "Kevin Corcoran" was just being himself and that self became the character of "Moochie," who was according to one of the *Disney* writers "part all-American boy and part hellion." (mr) A description that probably fit me also! Once again this points out "Moochie," Steve, not Kevin, "thinking in Moochie" and the complexity of that! GOT THAT! SO FAR?

Moochie of movie and TV, Kevin Corcoran, was born on June 10, 1949, six months and one day before my birth. He played in *Old Yeller, Toby Tyler, The Shaggy Dog, Swiss Family Robinson*, and *Pollyanna*, but he was most remembered for the recurring role of "Moochie" in *The Mickey Mouse Club, Spin and Marty*, and some in which he played the lead role, *Moochie of the Little League* and *Moochie of Pop Warner Football*. In the late 1950s and early 1960s, Kevin was one of the most visible child actors of that time. Kevin Corcoran was inducted into the *Disney Legends* in 2006. After playing Moochie and other roles, Kevin Corcoran became a director and producer on many films! He passed away on October 6, 2015. He was 66. The oldest Moochie living in captivity could now be me, currently at 68 (2018 until Dec 11, 2018).

Steven "Moochie" Knowles

Many thanks go to Marla Duncan (Doug's wife) for saying she had trouble understanding the way I write and inspiring me to put these rules out to, I hope, clear up the strangeness of Moochie talking, writing, and thinking. (mr) Doug Duncan who was not only the center on our basketball team but the tight end on our football team, and he was the State Record Holder for the javelin throw, AND he was Marla's husband, DUH, so needless to say, Doug was a very busy boy to say the least! (mr) Wow, this pair of "back to back" run-on sentences is Moochie's best grouping of run-on sentences EVER! Thanks also to the Steve, him, not the other Steve, me, for translating "Moochie" so Marla might understand it! GOT THAT! So far?

So if you happen to be talking to one of my classmates about me and call me by my real name, Steve, and they give you a look like, "Who the heck are you talking about? I remember Moochie doing that, but I'm sure Steeby never did that!" (mr) (By the way Steve Steeby was always called just "Steeby" for short by our classmates), forgive them, as to them Moochie was a live character in the play of my life.

Second grade

Third grade

Fourth grade—Moochie where is the camera?

Fifth grade

# The Box of
# Everything

# Chapter 1

The next three chapters stand together as adventures of the brothers after their arriving in Goddard. These three chapters span the early years in Goddard, 1956 to 1960.

This story could have had another title like THE ADVENTURES OF CHUCK AND STEVE. However, since it is inspired by THE BOX OF EVERYTHING, that is the title that seemed most appropriate.

The Knowles family came to Goddard in the summer of 1956. This was the greatest summer of my life to that point, but what do I know? I was six. Now, the family had a roster of seven and two adults, a Mom and a Dad. And like most families of the 1950s, divorce was not the "it" thing to do in small town Kansas, yet, anyway. The rest of the roster consisted of all boys. Yep, five boys that ranged in ages from two to twelve. I was the middle boy at six, or six and a half; every day counts when you are that age. I was the middle boy because someone had to be the referee between the two oldest, Jim and Chuck, and the two youngest, Bill and Bob, as they were the "twin terrors." Bill and Bob were at two years old or actually two and a half. Their birthday, like mine, was in December. They lived up to the "twin terror" label, as they were twins and they did inflict terror. Just ask Mike Murray, oops, Mike has passed on. Now the twins had nothing to do with that, but the terror the twins inflicted on Mike was sometimes comical, sometimes "devilish!" But Mike was a terror in his own right, ask anybody!

*Left to right—Moochie, Bill, Jim, Bob, and Chuck*

Jim was the oldest at twelve, while Chuck was the second oldest at nine. Both Jim and Chuck had their birthdays in the spring, so they were those ages without any need for fractions. Not to repeat myself, but yes, I was that boy in the middle. My real name is Steve, but most of my friends call me Moochie. We will get to the why of that later on. As you can tell, creativity in the naming of children had not been invented, yet. We were the normal family of seven that inhabited small Kansas towns in the 1950s, but it usually was with girls mixed in with boys. Goddard was so small that the town's census increased by about 5 percent with our moving in. Not sure if it affected the property value or not, but Dad and Mom bought that house in Goddard for just over $12,000. A dollar went a lot farther back then!

Goddard had a Main Street Business District of about two and a half blocks. I say about two and a half blocks, because Steeby's house and a couple of more houses would have to be included if it were three blocks long. Those houses were on the north end of the business district of Main Street. And as everybody knows, you don't have houses in the business district of Main Street!

The Steeby house and those others should have been bakeries or a sundries or something to do with a business. Nope, it was a few houses on Main Street that were in the north part of the business district! They call that prime real estate, now! So the three blocks became the two and a half blocks of the business district. But it was a small town! Goddard did not have zoning rules, yet!

A few days after we moved in, Mom and I took a walk to inspect the town. We walked the three blocks from Spruce Street to the Goddard Business District: all two and a half blocks of it! An eight block walk would put you "out of town" anywhere in Goddard! A thriving metropolis it was not!

*Mary Knowles*

During our walk Mom decided the first store to check out would be AF&A Market. It held all those items that she would need to keep five growing boys from becoming raging cannibals: food! So Mom and I walked the aisles of the store, scoping out where everything that mattered to Mom was and which shelf it was on; this Mom's stuff can get complex. Of course there was no attention made to things I might want to inspect, up close and personal like. This was Mom's inspection tour, and I was only along to learn the process, or because she didn't want to leave me with no adult supervision! Yep, I was that boy!

With the tour completed, we . . . no, Mom needed to buy something so it would make the trip look necessary. It didn't take long to find something to meet our . . . no, Mom's need, as I had no say in what was selected to be in that shopping cart. After securing Mom's choice . . . NOT mine, in the shopping cart, we proceeded to the checkout counter.

Well, before getting to the checkout, we had to go right by a bunch of shelves. On those shelves were candy bars of every kind, while Mom passed them by without seemingly to even notice them, but I DID NOTICE them! Those candy bars were right in front of me. It seemed like they were talking to me saying "Eat me, ooh pick me, eat me!" So I picked out one that looked like the chewiest, the most tasty, and stuffed it in my pocket.

After we left the store, we started our trek home, but after just a few steps, that candy bar started to burn a hole in my pocket. So I heeded its call and pulled it out. I undid its wrapper a little bit and bit into that chewy, delicious, "piece of heaven." Unfortunately, I had an audience. The next voice I heard was not the siren call of the candy bar but of a very angry Mom. "DROP YOUR DRAWERS, RIGHT NOW!" she said, VERY LOUDLY, I might add! So loudly that I was sure that everybody in the AF&A Market heard her. But no one came out of the store, and I was glad no one did because I knew what was about to happen.

Mom had rules, and the small ones broken would get a swat or two on the back side of the jeans. The big ones, when broken, would get hard swats on the bare bottom. Mom called this stealing, and she was not going to have a THIEF in her house! So it was the big one! Only lying held an equal punishment, as she was not going to have a LIAR there either! Thinking back on that, "Would I have received more punishment for stealing and lying about it or killing someone and telling the truth about it?" On second thought, I shudder to think if that would've been a time when Dad dealt out the punishment!

After the physical punishment was dealt, Mom proceeded to put other actions out that I was to obey OR ELSE! I didn't ask her what the "or else" meant. It could have meant another round with her hand striking my bare bottom or her telling Dad and me facing his wrath. Neither option appealed to me. I quietly awaited her further orders, which were I was going to go back into the store and tell the lady at the counter what I had done. I was to put the half-eaten candy bar in front of the lady along with a nickel that my Mother "loaned" to me, and she also stipulated how I would repay it. With Mom her "any loans" had something to do with dishes. I hated washing dishes, and Mom knew this!

After I had done my "sentence," the lady (who I found out later was the wife of the owner of the store, Wilbur Floyd), Mrs. Floyd, tried to help me out by blaming her husband for putting those candy bars on the bottom shelf where they would tempt small children.(mr) But Mom would have none of the excuses! When Mrs. Floyd tried to give me the remains of the candy bar, as with the nickel, Mrs. Floyd must have figured I owned that candy bar, but my Mom blocked the attempt with a motion to the trash can under the counter.(another mr?) One more part of the "sentence": I was not to gain anything from my crime. Mom had made her statement loud and clear not only to me but to the whole town. I'm sure the story made all the gossip that week in Goddard! And if it did not, it sure made an impression on me! And I still had a lot of dishes to wash! By the way, there wasn't a dish washing machine in most houses yet! It had to be done by hand, my hands!

Mom wasn't the only Knowles checking out the town. My brother, Chuck, and I were doing a little investigating on our own. At the end of the business district on the south end of Main was Whetzel Lumber. Across the street was Dennis Hardware. It was in Dennis Hardware that we found it: THE BOX OF EVERYTHING!

It was a simple wood box about three feet wide by about two feet. It was on a table that was about two feet high. The depth of the box was probably around four inches. Inside, the box was divided into squares of about four inches by four inches by thin wood slats that were used to separate the compartments. Inside of each compartment were items pertaining to an activity as old as the world itself: fishing! That box had everything needed to catch "the BIG ONE" or every size of fish that could be caught! It had hooks of all sizes, it had fishing lines on spools, it had plastic worms, it had bobbers, it had weights of all weights, and it had it all right there in that box! The Box of Everything!

It also had a card in every compartment that had written on it the price of the items in each compartment. And that price was written in a way all of us kids could understand: cents! Some things in the box could even be had for a single cent, better known to us kids as a penny. On other compartments it could have two cents each, while others had two for five cents, but it was always in kids'-type monetary language. Every business man had to know and understand his customers, and old man Dennis did KNOW his customers! The Box of Everything was pure genius in its simple approach to his customers: us! Just like the fish we hoped to catch, we were caught by it!

While I stood in front of the Box of Everything lost in my dream of catching that "big one," Chuck was taking another angle in his mind. How to get all those pennies that we needed to get what was before us in that box? You could almost feel the heat and smell the smoke of his mind as he assembled his plan! I was not sure how Chuck's mind worked, but if it meant that we could acquire the means to fund our fishing adventures, then to me, he was Andrew

Carnegie! (mr) Who? I didn't know but Chuck did, as he was always bringing him (whoever he was) up!

Now Chuck was in charge of the family mower. It was his job to cut the grass when it needed cutting. But no one said we couldn't offer our services to the neighbors. This worked for a while. Everything was right in the world; everybody was happy! Chuck and I were happy, and we visited the box almost every day buying the "tools of what we wanted to be our trade." That made old man Dennis happy. Yes, we did have to dodge the question of why the gas can seemed to always be empty with Dad having to buy more, but it was working.

Working, that is, until Chuck decided to check the mower's blade while it was running and ended up cutting the end of his thumb off! Okay, so Chuck was known as a very smart kid, but he lost two things that day: a bit of that reputation and the end of his thumb! That might have been the reason Dad started taking us with him to his work that summer. Mom might have thought we needed a little Dad type rearing up. Maybe a little early for Dad type of raising but . . . Now Dad was a heavy-duty diesel mechanic with a rep of being the best in his field, and Mid-Continent Construction would keep him on their payroll to ensure that the equipment was ready to head out to its next big job of laying pipelines.

Dad always used his kids as his "go-for" as in "get me a 7/16 wrench out of that tool box." He also used his work as a way to teach his kids "how to work," and that time was not only for the gage to get paid but also to "get something done while you are there!" At that time we kids thought it was his way to torture us! In truth it was his half of the parent thing; Mom is to guide us in "right or wrong" stuff, and Dad was to get us ready for "the world of work" thing. The key to surviving in the "Knowles" house was to know the "rules,"

Mom's big rules were never lie, cheat, or steal; Dad's one big rule, besides the "how to work" thing, was you never walk or stand in between him and the television set during *The Friday Night Fights!* When Dad was home working at the Mid-Continent Construction's shop, Friday nights became Dad's TV NIGHTS, and none of us kids challenged THAT! The shop, basically Dad's shop, was on South Hoover Road. It backed up to the "Big Ditch," and that is where the next chapter of our story begins.

# Chapter 2

Wichita, Kansas, was pretty much on a flat plain with very poor drainage. A flood was the normal result anytime it rained anything more than a dust settler. Preventing floods became imperative for life and businesses on the west side of Wichita. The city built a big ditch, also known by the fancier name Big Slough, to divert water around the west side of the city. It was about a hundred yards wide with the dirt dug from the base made into the hills that made the banks of the perimeter.

Most of the time it was pretty dry with a stream running down the middle of it. The soil was mostly sandy loam which made the perfect habitat for a creature that became what populated it or, as many would say, infested it: LIZARDS! There were two different types: the small brown sand lizard and the green and yellow lizard that we called the Mrs. Willard's.

We called them that because when we lived in Macksville, Kansas, we had a neighbor, the Willards, whose backyard was infested with them. Macksville was just one of many towns that we held residence in during Dad's time in the pipeline business. The "vagabond family" tells of all the twists and turns of that story!

The Mrs. Willard's lizards were bigger than the brown sand lizards and much more colorful. It wasn't long after we snuck away from Dad's shop and our duties when we saw the first lizard. While I chased it, Chuck was seeing dollar signs. This could be it!

Our mowing business was getting to be a lot like work and maybe dangerous. After watching me chase that elusive lizard with comical results, Chuck came up with a scheme to catch the lizards successfully and economically. To me those lizards were fun to chase. To Chuck those lizards were the key to acquiring all those things in the Box of Everything!

The first thing to solve was to come up with a way to catch the lizards. Chuck solved that with our favorite tool, our fishing poles. A fitting solution as most of our time was spent fishing or thinking about fishing. But now instead of using hooks to catch our prey, we would use the fishing line to catch them. Tying a loop in the line above the first eyelet of the pole would create a snare to catch the lizard, and we simply reeled them in.

With our poles and the length of our arms, the lizards would not know the danger until it was too late. As for keeping them while we went for more, Chuck decided on mason jars with holes in the lids so they could breathe. As long as we kept the lizards in shade, they would be fine in their new state of captivity. The first part of our new "lizard business" was well conceived, and in trial runs it worked really well.

The next part was sales. What would be our sales pitch? What would be the "why" our customers would buy what we wanted to sell to them? How should we make our product appeal to them? Actually, there really wasn't a "we," or an "us," but there was a Chuck. I let Chuck decide the answer to all of these questions as he was good at all the logistical things. Since there are two of us and Chuck is obviously the president, then I must be the number two in charge. I'm only six and a half years old, and chasing lizards is what I do best! Isn't that what all VPs in the world do?

He had all that covered and all the organizational things covered, too. Like I said, that is what he was good at! I was the doer: he'd tell me what to do and how to do it, and I would do it! I was the "tagalong," the sidekick; Chuck was the Lone Ranger, and I was his Tonto! When Chuck called a "brainstorming idea meeting," I would listen to all of his ideas and proceeded to do my part of Chuck's ideas. They seemed to be always better than my "not having any ideas," ideas!

Now, Moochie hadn't been born yet. In fact, I hadn't met Steve Steeby who started the story of Moochie. But I could hear Moochie scurrying around up there in my head. "What a mess; are you going to clean that up?" I would get used to it; Moochie would leave a mess everywhere he went! Somebody should have hired a maid to follow him around, as the Joker (in Batman) would later say, with a small change, from "me" to "him," "Wait until they get a load of him!"

Here's what we (Chuck) decided; we would market the lizards as "cute" pets that could go everywhere with the customer. In fact each lizard would have a string tied to its foot and a safety pin tied to the other end. The safety pin could be attached to their shirt. Each lizard could ride along with its owner! The plan sounded really great; he was good at that marketing thing, too. I'm still chasing that first lizard, and Chuck was designing a business plan. We were going to be rich!

As far as price Chuck said, he thought the little brown sand lizards should bring a dime, while the more colorful green and yellow (Mrs. Willard's) should bring a quarter. Whoa, we had just started, and we were now talking about dimes and quarters! No more pennies and nickels for us! Chuck even had an idea for taking the smaller brown sand lizards in trade so that customers could move up to the Mrs. Willard's lizard. Whoa, we were going to dominate the used brown lizard market, too!

The "lizard business" was all set to go! All we needed to do was to catch the "product," the lizards, and then start the second phase: the selling! The fishing pole loop thing worked great, and soon we had enough lizards of each type to open our store. The store wasn't actually a building with windows and sales desks. It was more a "territory" which was Spruce Street, our street. We could start on Spruce Street where we knew the "customers," the kids, and refine our sales technique.

Take the lessons which we had learned from old man Dennis and his "Box of Everything." Get inside the hopes and dreams of our customers, just like the "Box of Everything" did with our hopes and dreams of fishing. Become the partner in making their hopes and dreams reality by providing the tools to do so. Just listening to Chuck explain all the ins and outs of "real" business told me that we were in good hands with his leading us. We were going to be rich!

Just like old man Dennis did with his "Box of Everything" with us and our hopes and dreams, we could be the "Box of Everything" to our customers (more Chuck talk). By learning what we were taught, we could move our target to Walnut Street on the west and Pine Street on the east. Each should be a success if it followed the rule of repetition (more Chuck); repeating successful plans brings success! I may not have known what that meant, but Chuck did and that was what mattered! Chuck was great with all the "know how and why stuff." And he could explain it to me, with all the complicated language of business talk stuff. It didn't matter if I understood it; Chuck did, and he told me. I just kept nodding my head in agreement with everything Chuck said.

Unfortunately there was a problem we had not addressed yet. It was one of those little things that we didn't even realize until it happened and wrecked everything.

*What would happen if all of those lizards happened to work their way loose from their bonds?*

Who would all the moms of Spruce Street blame when they came upon an unwelcome visitor in their home? Does anyone believe that those rightful owners would take the blame? Of course not, our phone started ringing, and unfortunately Mom started answering it. Soon our scheme to get rich was out in the open.

But unlike all those that pointed their finger at Chuck and me, we never tried to lay blame on old man Dennis. He was just following sound business practices (more Chuck talk), for having the Box of Everything as the first thing one would see upon entering his store. Old man Dennis was a great guy, and neither Chuck nor I would let any blame be passed on to anyone except us.

We knew what we were doing. We were not too young to know (okay maybe I was) the difference between right and wrong! In the "Knowles house," you better know right from wrong; the penalty for not knowing was too painful! But was it wrong or just an unforeseen result of possible sabotage by jealous persons known or unknown? Who did untie the lizards? Chuck should have been a lawyer as he could "argue" our side in detail; of course Chuck never did the arguing (more Chuck talk), he would tell me what to say and I would "argue" our opinion . . . what's that Chuck . . . not our opinion, but what . . . I can't hear you with your hand over your mouth . . . Chuck always seemed to put me in charge of explaining to others what Chuck said . . . we were a team after all, and Chuck left that to me . . . and it did make me feel big . . . and that was my part!

Most of what we speculated was not the money maker we envisioned it to be. But we did sell some lizards to the kids in Goddard. We sold enough to continue to visit the Box of Everything many times. We may not have been the best customers of Dennis Hardware, but we may have been the most liked by old man Dennis, which was important to Chuck and me. He never failed to take that walk on those creaky floors to meet us at the box, calling out to us as he got near, "Gonna catch the big one today, boys!" Looking back at those days, I think old man Dennis probably had that hardware store for something to do as he was "old," and he must have loved kids. I guess he created that "Box of Everything" just for the looks on a kid's face as they stood in front of it, dreaming and fishing in their minds! That box was all about kids and the genius of pricing in "cents" was "priceless!" For Chuck and me, it was the reason we made that "long" trek to his store as often as we could. With a few pennies in our pockets, we could dream.

That adventure was neither the first nor the last for us Knowles boys. We moved on to other creatures that slithered or swam or burrowed or flew. It was just something we did! It was the P.T. Barnum guy (yeah more Chuck stuff) that we should try to be like! What's that Chuck, a sucker gets born how often?

## Chapter 3

# The Six-Foot Bull Snake

Our dreams of riches were dashed, either by a bunch of resourceful lizards or maybe by someone jealous of our "inventive spirit." Or maybe it was laziness in handling the responsibility of taking care of the lizards. Or it might have been all Chuck's and my fault. But there are some indisputable facts: the lizards did get loose, and the moms of Spruce Street did get a little irate! Now the questioning of Mom's ability to keep her sons in check went a little too far. Mom's place in our family was not that of "drill sergeant."

Mom knew absolutely nothing about what Chuck and I were up to in the lizard business. But if Mom would have known, I don't believe she would have squashed it from its inception but rather, with her "smarts," as she was an incredibly smart person, she probably would have foreseen the probability of this happening and made a list of guidelines for us to follow (mr). She would probably have required we sell homes for the lizards, places to put them when they weren't hanging off of a customer's shirt. Of course the cost would have skyrocketed, and many of our customers would have been "priced out of the market"(Chuck speaks again). It would have eliminated the dime as the basement price and probably made the lowest price a quarter.

Mom had pretty much squashed our lizard business with a declaration of "No more lizards, PLEASE." But Chuck and I took that to mean "for now" as she did say "please" at the end. We decided to put the lizard business "on hold" for now. Within a week we, were in the "snake business" as we had been "eyeballing" a large bull snake that lived under our propane tank in our backyard. Chuck went about building a cage. Chuck asked me how big I thought it was. Whoa, Chuck was asking ME a question. Of course I had no idea, but I shot back, "At least six foot!" So it became the six-foot bull snake!

Now Chuck was using my "estimation" as a size to build the cage. Most bull snakes are either all coiled up or laying out "sunning" themselves as our resident snake handler, Chuck, had decided. So he determined that the cage be three feet by one and a half feet. It was the half length of the snake in width by one-quarter length of the snake in depth of the cage rule! The complexity caused me to believe there was such a rule, besides that Chuck was always coming up with complex stuff that seemed right to me!

Now the real question came up; all the real questions with Chuck were about money. With a snake so large, how could we make money off of it? Chuck had held the position of "snake expert," so any answer out of his mouth was going to be what we were going to do. If he said we could chop it and sell the pieces, I would have gone into the kitchen to get a butcher knife. Chuck thought for a while and then answered with pure genius.

"A snake this large will eat probably a couple times a day, maybe more. Let's sell seats to watch the snake eat! Round up lawn chairs, folding chairs, and any other chairs we can find. This time we are going to be rich!" A thought came into my head which does not happen very often; what do snakes eat? Chuck responded with a simple but thoughtful answer, "Anything it wants!" The "anything" was simple, and the "it wants" part caused us to think. It came down to something that we had plenty of; a little more thinking brought us to the sparrows that seemed abundant in Goddard. How do we "secure" that food supply? BB guns! Both Chuck and I had BB guns, and we had plenty of BBs.

Chuck got the cage for the bull snake built, and it was beautiful! At least as beautiful as a prison for a snake can be. It was built to the specifications that Chuck had determined for a snake of his size. All we needed now was the snake. Now catching snakes was maybe one of Chuck's best skills. He had been known to leap to the ground and catch a snake by its tail just before it disappeared down its hole. So a snake in broad daylight had almost no chance of escaping even if was partially hidden by a propane tank. After a few lunges, the snake was ours!

Sparrows must not be the smartest of birds. They will, or another sparrow will, just fly and land on a telephone wire that just had a sparrow shot off it just moments before. So if you are hunting sparrows and you want three, you can pretty much do so without moving. The nice thing about BB guns is that most of the time you only stun the sparrows and not kill them. This is not only nice for the bull snake as they prefer their prey alive but also for drama when the stunned bird wakes up facing a hungry snake.

Didn't think about how cruel that might be to the sparrow, but it did bother me later. I think most of our audience, the kids who paid a nickel to watch the "drama," hadn't thought about it at first either. But when they started leaving before the last sparrow was eaten, it was pretty evident that one show was all that the "kids" could take.

The six-foot bull snake idea had ended as a bust. The nickels that we had received, and that we didn't have to refund to the unhappy audience members, were the only nickels we would be getting from *that* "drama." But it did give us a reason to visit the Box of Everything in Dennis Hardware the next day! And Chuck sold the snake to Mike Murray who lived a few houses down. Nobody knows what Mike did with the snake. After watching the snake eat, I really think that nobody cared what Mike did with it either.

So our first snake business adventure was a loser, but there were more snakes for us to catch, make that for Chuck to catch, and for us to make money on. The next to enter as our star attraction was the hog nose snake. Now there was an actor! Move over Marlon Brando, the best performance of an actor in a lead role goes to "Mister Hog Nose!"

When the hog nose is first threatened, it goes into the first act as being the meanest snake alive. It hisses, it spits, and it even puffs up like the deadly "puff adder" snake. Also the "puffing up" made the hog nose snake seem a lot bigger. If the threat does not go away after that, then the hog nose goes into the next act of flattening its neck making it look like a deadly cobra. Then if the threat does not go away, it turns over and flops on its back and plays dead! Top that Brando!

Unfortunately, it did finish the act by defecating all over itself. In doing so it released the most awful-smelling substance ever held in the bowels of a living creature! No creature could have stayed within twenty feet of that finish and that included us. We let the best act go after that! We let it slither away that night to perform its Oscar-deserving act somewhere else. If we want an act to play dead, let's get an opossum next time; I don't think it poops all over itself as a finale.

Now there were other candidates for us to catch and sell like the blue racer and its cousin the Western racer. But after catching them, we found them to be not only very fast but also one of the meanest snakes with a very bad disposition!

With the circumstances that we remembered from our "lizard business," it would not be smart to bring not only a very fast snake but one that seemed to go out of its way to show its displeasure for being held in captivity. If it got loose in Goddard, does anybody think that the Spruce Street moms would not blame us? So we chose not to sell the very beautiful, in color, blue racer or the Western racer.

So we chose the "docile" garter snake. They were plentiful and easy to catch. At our first sales event with the "tame" snake, Chuck told me to show our first customers, the McColley sisters, Doreen and Jeannie, how docile and how tame the snakes were. So I dropped one of our "tame" snakes inside my shirt.

Well sometimes the best-laid plans go horribly wrong, and this was one of those times! Inside my shirt, the snake found a soft spot and buried those tiny teeth into the flesh of my stomach. I pulled up my shirt in a panic! Doreen McColley, who was Chuck's age, took a look at that snake which was firmly attached to my stomach and said, "It won't let go until it thunders!" I looked up to behold a beautiful blue sky without a cloud in sight!

No matter how much talking Chuck did, I was not going to demonstrate ever again how this or that was worth a customer investing their nickels, or pennies, in Chuck's businesses. If he wants someone to do it, let him be the demonstrator!

So Chuck decided on another business where we wouldn't be selling to the kids of Spruce Street but to another interested buyer, big John McCammon. John McCammon had decided to offer worms for people who wanted them for fishing bait as a part of his gas station inventory. It was kind of like adding a bait shop to his empire there on 54 Highway. The town of Goddard was just northeast of Lake Afton and about twenty minutes from Cheney Lake, which was northwest of Goddard. So being on the way to those lakes and selling live bait should have been a successful venture.

We would get a penny for every worm! So we went into the worm business! Now, this was THE business that we would get rich doing! Or so we thought. We already knew of a place to get the worms; it was under the mulberry tree about a block over on Walnut. That was where we had dug up many worms to do our own fishing. Now I should have realized when I was the only one carrying a shovel who was going to do the digging and who was the one to do the counting of the worms. That was okay because we were a team!

Now the worm business didn't last very long because either we had used up many of the worms under the mulberry tree for our own fishing excursions or because it was hot and the worms must have gone a little deeper. I didn't know that worms went deeper, but Chuck said they did. Chuck decided that was the reason and digging deeper seemed more like work, and we always stayed away from what we called work!

I never asked Chuck if it was my digging, or him counting, was what we called work! But it does get hot in the summers in Kansas, and that summer it got hotter than normal, so I bought the reasons. Although the heat may have caused the end of our worm business, moneywise we did pretty well! And we did take a couple trips to the Box of Everything with the profits from our successful venture into the world of worms!

We did have another "get rich scheme" in the last days of our childhood, Chuck's childhood that is, as at about fifteen in our family meant going to work in the summer. Chuck was getting close to that number! Learning how to work was considered a part of life, and it was an expected thing in our family!

But in 1960 when Chuck was thirteen and I was ten and a half, our partnership was getting close to its end. One last attempt for the "gold ring" of success was going to be the last gasp before real work would take Chuck away. He was already feeling the pressure as Dad had bought the Derby Gas Station at Highway 54 and Main Street, and

Chuck was already performing minor duties at Dad's gas station. There must have been no child labor laws at that time.

There was an old trailer behind the gas station, and since it was on Dad's property, we claimed it. I don't remember how we got the fireworks and the authorization to open up a fireworks stand, but Chuck went ahead and started measuring and designing a structure that would make that trailer a fireworks stand. So Chuck or Dad must have handled those parts of getting the fireworks, as that detail had slipped from my memory.

The firecracker trailer had many of those things that made it a candidate for a likeable way to make money and to have fun while doing it! It was a business that, unlike the garter snake fiasco, I would volunteer to give demonstrations to our customers. Which I did many times!

Chuck designed the structure to be an "A" frame-type fireworks stand. One side of the trailer was the low point, and the other side was the high point. Stair-stepped shelves with bottom being the largest shelf and the top shelf being the smallest would make up the display area. There were also shelves on both sides; the more front shelves the better. The fireworks were displayed at the front of the shelves, with the stock of the fireworks waiting to move up to be displayed placed behind the displayed fireworks.

The angled sides were ¾-inch plywood, as were the back and the front, which was the door that opened from the bottom and held by hinges at the top. It also locked at the bottom. It was a great design. The trailer was pulled by a 1926 Dodge car that Dad had bought at an auction. And

Chuck both drove it from its stall and backed it back to its stall when the day of selling fireworks ended.

Although Chuck did not have a driver's license, as he was only thirteen, he was mature enough to perform that small task very well. Dad had okayed it as Chuck was getting close to the age that Dad would start teaching him how to drive, and this could be the beginning of that process. The fireworks stand didn't raise much money, but Chuck and I had a lot of fun demonstrating all the various items we had for sale!

What would come next was to bring more manpower to the "Knowles Boys Corporation," as younger brothers Bill and Bob had shown a lot of promise in our endeavors! Although Mom still thought of them as her babies, both Chuck and I had faith that we could corrupt them as they entered the Knowles Boys . . . obviously at the ground level.

But Chuck would be leaving next year to join the working mass. And in serious matters like ideas and the knowhow to put those (his) ideas in a presentable way to make the, not pennies now, dimes and quarters, Chuck was the key! The Knowles Boys would not only need members to step up in the ranks to fill the void but also the idea guy. All corporations and organizations need new blood, and the Knowles Boys were no exception, but there was no one to replace the brains of the Knowles Boys Corporation. When Chuck left for the "world of work," unfortunately his smarts left with him! Just don't expect Steve (me) or Moochie (also me) to move into the spot. I am just the "sidekick," the "tagalong," and the "doer" waiting for the "to do" instructions of what to do. I was the one who inspired ALL with his comedic chasing of lizards! Not the leader, but the follower, the comedic relief, maybe? "Will Bill or Bob please turn out the lights, we're done here!"

# The Vagabond Family

# Chapter 1

This story is of the Knowles family and the many twists of life during and after its vagabond start. The next two chapters are of that story.

Webster's Dictionary: Vagabond, n., idle wanderer, tramp. We were not idle nor tramps, but we certainly were wanderers; we moved around a lot.

There was a time period of the Knowles family when it had a "move about" nature. Well that could be a reputation very well deserved! I was only six when we moved to Goddard, and before that we had either lived in or at least travelled through twenty three states! My Dad was kind of like the Paladin character in *Have Gun—Will Travel*, but he didn't wear a gun or have a fast draw. He was like a hired gun, though, as he had a special talent that pipeline construction companies crave, so he did a lot of that "traveling." And, by extension, so did the rest of the Knowles family.

Now, all during my early life and even before there was a "me," a job completed meant packing up and moving to a new location. For Jim, and later Chuck, it meant changing schools. Since we moved so very often, it meant losing friendships just developing for Jim and Chuck. How does a mother tell her kids not to make friends because they'll lose them soon? It was very tough to live the vagabond life! In fact, even Mom had lost friends, but at least she knew it was the life she was stuck with at that time. However, she had to have thoughts about having a permanent address, a real home for the family.

My oldest brother, Jim, said he had at least a dozen and possibly as many as fifteen different schools that he attended from kindergarten through the sixth grade! There were also at least five different states for all the cities and towns that Mom, Dad, and, starting in 1944, their ever-growing family called home, at least for a while. Jim also said about those times from 1950, when he started school, up to 1956, when Mom and Dad finally bought the house in Goddard that he never started and finished a grade at any "one school." This was because the Knowles family moved during the school year at least once every year!

There were four different states in which schools were involved in the moving! The towns before the kids were in school were Rupert, Idaho, which was Jim's birthplace, and Burley, Idaho, which was Chuck's birthplace three years later. The added problem of dealing with schools started in 1950. Being moved from and enrolling in a different school became the norm of the vagabond life. The places spanned from Richmond, Virginia, to Chillicothe, Missouri, to Ottumwa, Iowa, and the many small towns in Kansas. Bucklin, Macksville, El Dorado, Emporia, Great Bend, and Wichita were among those places. Some towns had schools that Jim had to enroll in twice because we moved back to that town later!

How does a person become wanted so badly in one field of employment? By becoming the best and, for most of his life, being willing to travel were two of the reasons why my Dad became so wanted by the pipeline industry. How he became the "best" in the field of heavy-duty diesel mechanic was started early in Dad's life.

Dad's interest in anything mechanical started on Grandpa Knowles' farm near Bucklin, Kansas. It started with an engine block that was being used as a fence weight. A fence weight was what farmers used to hold down fences in a gully of a stream to keep cows in the pasture that they should be in. That engine block was the starting point of Dad learning "what makes an engine run!" So he cleaned it up and "made it shine," as he used to say about cleaning anything. All of the pistons, plugs and pans, and everything else could be added later to that engine block. To make an internal combustion engine run, all those parts are needed. So after absorbing a "tongue lashing" for taking the weight from the fence, Dad was able to make the engine start. He was twelve years old! The passion had already started being all consuming when that engine "fired up" or in ordinary terms "it started!"

A few years later while "cranking the crank" to start an engine, Dad suffered a blow that broke his knee cap as the crank kicked back when the engine fired. It was an enormously painful injury; he would live in pain, but he recovered. With FDR's plan to get people back to work, Dad enlisted into the Civilian Conservation Corp (CCC). The CCC built roads and lakes in our country during the thirties. Of course it was heaven to Dad with all those tractors, trenchers, and other big machinery all around him. Those big machines needed a mechanic, and he was to learn the trade that he would become known as "the best" at!

The injury that he had suffered years before kept him from active military service, but he was in the place where he belonged. After getting a lot of his "on the job training" working on the equipment with the CCC, Dad started his "move about" early period. A "homesick" wife had a lot to do with that start, not my Mom, but Mom's brother Lon's wife, Retha. So Lon was going to move to Idaho where Retha called home. So it began, the move about period.

Being young and not yet tied down by a family, Mom and Dad decided to go along. Dad and Lon started a mechanic shop in Heyburn, Idaho. So the first move of many, many more was about a young wife getting home-sick. So the "move about" life really didn't start because Dad was the best. He didn't have that reputation, yet. Something like that takes time and in the right setting; on the pipeline is where it has to be "made."

So after a fire burned down the Burley Tractor where Dad was working, he and Mom decided it was time to return to Kansas. It was the late forties, so Dad, Mom, a couple of small boys, Jim and Chuck, started back to Kansas. Dad went to work at Foley Tractor in Dodge City, Kansas. I was born in December of 1949. Dad had become a heavy-duty diesel mechanic of note by that time. With the experience at both Burley and Foley Tractor, he was more than qualified to work on tractors, especially Caterpillar tractors. Caterpillar was the brand of tractor most used in the pipeline industry.

After a while he was offered a top-paying job as a heavy-duty diesel mechanic by a pipeline construction company which he accepted. The vagabond family started on the trek where Dad became the most wanted person among the troop of vagabonds. That troop followed the industry that laid the pipes in the ground through which the oil and natural gas that America ran on flowed!

Now some men followed gold strikes, oil strikes, or, in some cases, just the availability of work. Dad was a little bit different. After his reputation was built in the early years on the pipeline, he didn't follow the pipeline; it seemed like it chased him! It seemed it would not let him go! He was an asset a pipeline company wanted and needed, and he had the reputation of being the best! He was the heavy-duty diesel mechanic that could keep a fleet of pipe laying equipment running so they could get that pipe in the ground.

Every piece of equipment must be maintained, and if it breaks down, it has to be fixed or the pipeline stops. Dad gave a pipeline construction company the ability to continue without a stop. His truck was like a shop on wheels. Dad had dozens of specialty wrenches and tools to work on these tractors. Because without them, and Dad, it would mean hauling it back to the dealer's shop to get it fixed. Dad had tools that only he knew what they were and where they were used. It was because he had personally made them or had them made to work on a specific piece of equipment.

Dad didn't work just for the money but also because he loved the work and the challenge of it! He did command the top wage for a heavy-duty diesel mechanic, but he was worth a lot more than that! Dad had what many said was "God-given-type talent." He could listen to an engine run and tell where it was "hurting." He was a diesel engine's best friend; he was its "doctor," and I never heard of him "misdiagnosing" any sick tractor!

It seemed like every pipeline company knew when one of Dad's jobs was ending, and the phone would start ringing. We called those periods "answering the bell." Dad did not have a resume all typed up and "neat like." He never filled out a job application. Every pipeline construction company knew his name, and "the best" was always a part of his reputation!

It was the job, wherever that was, where Dad was king! Even though Dad loved his family, his world revolved around his work. He was worse than an "alcoholic"; he was worse than a "workaholic!" He was consumed in the challenges of the job and his drive to be called the best. He tried many times to stay at home, but the work around a shop seemed to bore him: no challenge in it. So the bell kept ringing, and I believe that Mom finally said, "Okay. Go ahead and answer that bell." And she probably added, "But the kids and I are staying here!"

That is when Dad relented, and they bought the house in Goddard. If he was going to keep answering the bell when it rang, Goddard would be as good of a place as any to be his base of operation. In fact, I think Dad was relieved, as now there were seven in the family and just up and moving to another location would be much more difficult. It had been difficult, but with five children in school, it would be almost impossible! So the vagabond family settled into life not on the road but in a new town, Goddard! It would be home.

It must have been the summer between Jim's eighth grade and his freshman year that Jim became interested in electronics. Dad evidently noticed that, and after finding out that Jim was serious about learning electronics, Dad ordered a home-study course from Devry on electronics. Dad even took it one step farther; he would also take the course with Jim. That might have been to verify to himself that Jim's interest was real and not just "anything but a mechanic"-type interest. If it was, Dad's money would have been wasted. As I could not see Dad wanting or needing to learn another trade, I think maybe he had other motives, maybe Jim?

Jim would be entering his freshman year. Maybe it was Dad's way of "opening doors" for one of his sons to find out what they wanted to do as a career. It could have been that, and if it was, Dad was right! Jim would later prove how right Dad had been, as Jim would become a top-notch "computer technician" after moving to California, but that would be in the future.

During the summer of the following year when Jim had turned fifteen, he was old enough to go along with Dad. I don't know if Mom okayed it. But Dad did as he evidently offered Jim a job, because when Dad left, Jim went with him. It was summer, so Jim could spend that "idle" time of summer with Dad and earn money at the same time! I don't think Jim knew that there was no "idle" time with Dad! My guess, it was really a way for Dad to get Jim "ready for the world of work." Jim must have thought that it was going to be an adventure. But I believe it was Dad's way to show Jim an incredible pace what the "world of work" demanded.

The first son is always a question mark to a Dad. But I believe by this time Dad knew Jim didn't have the desire needed to follow in Dad's footsteps. But Dad still wanted Jim to be the "best" at whatever he chose to do, and he did come down pretty hard on Jim. Jim, after a month or so, complained in a phone call to Mom "that no matter when they stopped work the day before, they always started the next day at 5:00 a.m.!" And Dad was famous for long days! So the day started early and ended late! Dad, it seemed, had to finish whatever he was working on, and that would be a "day!" I would later take that attitude into my carpenter work, but that would also be in the future. Dad did not want his oldest son "soft" toward work, so he set the bar high, maybe too high.

Maybe the best way to describe Dad's parenting style was what Johnny Cash would later say in the song *A Boy Named Sue*. The line that described it best is "so I gave you that name and said goodbye, I knew you'd have to get tough or die." That might "sum up" Dad's philosophy on raising kids. Real "caveman" stuff, but that was Dad, "I don't have time to teach you what you need to know, so here it is, learn it!" He didn't explain; he didn't even say what "it" was! It was like "I learned 'it' on my own, so learn 'it'!" But what is "it?" We never got an answer.

So Jim came home after that job; he had survived. But I don't believe he ever got Dad to explain what "it" was, but Jim probably did learn "it" on his own. I guess Dad got what he wanted, and Jim "got tough and did not die" but survived. Jim also made money as going along with Dad did not give anyone time to spend it. Dad was so consumed by what he had become that I think he dreamed about work. I later got that way, too.

I'm not sure how much money Jim brought back, but he did spend a lot on the "boys" that he had left behind, his four brothers, during his "adventure." He bought me a twelve-foot "pole vaulting pole," or it could have been for me and Chuck. Both of us had developed a desire to throw ourselves into the air without a thought of the "danger!" Chuck would take that desire to set the eighth grade record for pole vaulting. The next year after that, I would set the seventh grade record for pole vaulting. But I never did break Chuck's eighth grade record. No matter how hard I tried, I just could not do it.

Jim also bought both Bill and Bob their own bicycles! It seemed like the right thing to do between brothers! Jim had gone through the fire of Dad's parenting and was glad to be home! Even without Jim's gifts to the brothers, we would have been very happy just to have him home. The gifts didn't matter; it was the brothers that mattered, and we five boys were together again!

We Knowles boys might have had different views and opinions of Dad and his parenting skills. He might have been tough on us. But like dads everywhere being misunderstood by their children comes with the territory of dads. The dads were in charge of the dad's stuff in raising the kids. A song that says a lot about dads everywhere that says so much is the following:

*Left to right—Bob, Jim, Chuck, Dad, Bill, and Moochie*

In the Living Years
Mike and the Mechanics

Every generation
Blames the one before
And all of the frustrations
Come beating on your door

I know that I'm a prisoner
To all my Father held so dear
I know that I'm a hostage
To all his hopes and fears
I just wish I could have told him in the living years

Oh, crumpled bits of paper
Filled with imperfect thought
Stilted conversations
I'm afraid that's all we've got

You say you just don't see it
He says it's perfect sense
You just can't get agreement
In this present tense
We all talk a different language
Talking in defense

Say it loud (say it loud), say it clear (say it clear)
You can listen as well as you hear
It's too late (it's too late) when we die (Oh, when we die)
To admit we don't see eye to eye

So we open up a quarrel
Between the present and the past
We only sacrifice the future
It's the bitterness that lasts

So don't yield to the fortunes
You sometimes see as fate
It may have a new perspective On a different date
And if you don't give up, and you don't give in
You may just be O.K.

Say it loud, say it clear
You can listen as well as you hear
It's too late when we die
To admit we don't see eye to eye

I wasn't there that morning
When my Father passed away
I didn't get to tell him
All the things I had to say

I think I caught his spirit
Later that same year
I'm sure I heard his echo
In my baby's new born tears
I just wish I could have told him in the living years

Say it loud, say it clear
You can listen as well as you hear
It's too late when we die
To admit we don't see eye to eye

Written by Bo Robertson and Mike Rutherford 1988, this song (poem) reaches down inside of all of us. It also seemed right that the group singing is "Mike and the Mechanics"; Dad was a mechanic, the best!

# Chapter 2

Jim would graduate from high school at Goddard in 1962. For the last six years that was a total of only "one" school! Quite a change from the first six years of never spending more than a couple of months at any "one" school! Jim went to Emporia State for a year, and then the wanderlust must have returned. Because he decided the Marines needed him, as they needed "a few good men," Jim would join the Marines in the fall of 1964. I guess he figured that since he had survived Dad's "boot camp" he could handle anything. By the middle of 1965, he was in Vietnam. I think he might have come to the conclusion that when people are trying to kill you, Dad's "boot camp" was pretty tame in comparison. I had heard before that soldiers would never talk about their bad experiences in war. Well the other four brothers got an earful one night in a "sports bar" almost forty years after it happened.

My youngest son, Marc, joined the Army shortly after 9/11. He was involved in that race from Kuwait to Baghdad. Being that Marc was the one to set up the "communications satellite receiver" . . . in other words, he had the "phone for his unit." The five brothers would meet at the "sports bar," and Marc would call my phone. It would be 3:00 a.m. "over there." After Marc and I would talk, I would pass the phone to one of the other brothers. Of course, after a brother would finish his talk with Marc, that brother would buy a round of beers for the brothers.

Something in Jim's talk with Marc struck something inside of Jim. Jim was back in the jungles of Vietnam. He was remembering an ambush and "fire fight." Jim was the "rocket man" for his platoon. "Rocket men" are usually singled out as they carry the mortar used to keep the enemy at bay. They usually are killed within the first ten seconds in a fire fight. For some reason, Jim lived through those ten seconds. What he witnessed, as all but three Marines of Jim's platoon died that day in the jungle, was what he relived that night in the "sports bar." He knew all of his Marine "brothers" by name and relived the way they died. It was a horrific story, one that after Jim's telling of it none of the brothers even spoke for a while as Jim was not only telling the story but reliving the horrors of it. We just sat there, not talking. I don't know how Jim and the other Marines got out. It wasn't something you talk about. I didn't want to possibly send Jim back to those jungles. I am even worried about Jim reading this.

After his tour of Vietnam, Jim was sent on a NATO-simulated war games exercise in Norway. Vietnam was over a hundred degrees, and Norway was the opposite as it was "freezing." Jim just couldn't get a break!

After his service in the Marine Corps, Jim went to Durham, North Carolina, as Dad's brother, Bill, was in the glass business in Durham. Jim took a job where Uncle Bill's wife worked at a motel. Jim would be the "troubleshooter fix it man" at that motel. It might have been a period of where Jim had to get his head "right" after his military service.

After a few months at that job, he was contacted by one of Dad's old friends, Bill Woods. Bill Woods was putting together a testing crew for a relatively new type of pipeline testing. He wanted people he could trust. They had to be smart, and they had to know how to work. Now he had known Dad for many years, and he also knew the two oldest Knowles boys. I'm sure he thought that they fit the requirements perfectly. So he contacted Chuck first and offered him one of the jobs; Chuck accepted! With Chuck already committed to the job, he went after Jim knowing how the Knowles boys liked to stick together. Knowing Chuck would be working with him, Jim also accepted.

I'm sure Bill Woods was happy as the testing crew was coming together with people that fit his requirements. Since it was to be a three-man crew, all that was needed was one more man. After finding that man, Bill Woods' testing crew was ready to start testing! This testing was called "hydrostatic testing" as it dealt with water being forced into the pipe until it reached a "pressure" that the pipe would either have a "blowout" or passing grade. This would deem its ability to safely hold what the pipeline had to carry, which in this case was natural gas. So Jim and Chuck would be working together testing the pipelines.

So in 1968 both Jim and Chuck would work with the same company as Dad. But Jim and Chuck worked independently of Dad. Jim and Chuck were two-thirds of the testing crew! It was one of the most important phases of pipeline construction. What moves through pipelines is not only very valuable, but it is also very dangerous. No one wants a leaky pipe, especially one with natural gas in it. A leak in a natural gas line could cause explosive gas pockets to form that could cause the loss of life due, not only, to an explosion but also due to the inhaling the gas. And the cost of repairing an existing pipeline is also staggering! So the testing of the pipes is very important on many levels!

Since innocent lives were at risk, higher standards were set by which the pipeline construction company had to follow to prevent that "leaky pipe" from happening. Strength specifications would be higher in urban areas and in certain areas, like bridges and under highways where they would sometimes have "double-wall' pipes. Each time a pipeline was tested, it was filled with water until the pressure set to those new specifications was met, a twenty-four-hour watch started where the pressure is constantly monitored. Any drop in pressure would mean a leak being detected and would stop the test. Then the process to find the leak and repair it starts. After which the testing starts once more. After passing the test, a mechanical device, called a "pig," would then push the water out of the pipe doing most of the necessary cleaning of the pipe, also.

I'm sure Dad had to be happy with "his" boys for showing they had learned the most important element of his teaching. Even though he would never show it or tell them that. They knew how to work hard and were not afraid of getting dirty while doing it!

It was near the end of the job when Jim and Chuck were on a twenty-four-hour watch cycle that an unexpected event happened. They had a wreck while driving a little too fast on rain-soaked pavement while "chasing the mechanical 'pig'." They were trying to get to the other end of the pipe so they could retrieve the "pig." They were on the twenty-four-hour watch, so they might have been a little tired and not as sharp as they usually were.

After a hospital stay Chuck came home to Kansas from the job with the pipeline company with some job experience and some broken bones, too! Jim returned to Durham, North Carolina, to heal from his with the same results as Chuck, broken bones and all. But Jim had other things on his mind. We would find out later what was on his mind!

After healing up, Jim went on a trip to Mexico and brought back to Kansas a wife, Bobbie! They rented a small house in Nashville, Kansas. Mom and Dad had bought a house in Nashville a little over a year earlier. I used to tell people during those times that after I moved out (left the nest), I came back to Goddard and found the Methodist Minister living in our house! This wasn't exactly true as I had helped them move after the Methodist Church had bought the house. But it seemed like a good story to satisfy the "why did you move?" question. As Sgt. Schultz of Hogan's Heroes always says, "I know nothing; I know nothing."

So in a kind of reversal of roles as Jim had always taken the hard job of dealing with problems as the oldest, it would be time for the other brothers to step up for him. With younger brothers Bill and Bob still in school there, the newlyweds would have people around that they knew. As Bobbie was also in high school, she would have some friends and relatives there also. Jim and Bobbie stayed about a year, and the vagabond bug must have hit Jim again, as he and Bobbie started on a "move about" period of their own. It ended up, after a few stops, in California.

I don't know if Jim ever thought about that course from Devry during his own "move about" period, but it did come in handy. That time spent taking the home-study course about electronics proved to be very valuable. It would give Jim the head start he needed in his "computer" career. It was with Dad, paid for by Dad, and I believe it was a way to help one of his boys, without being seen as doing it. Jim was able to add to the Devry home-study course with a study on computers in classes at "Control Data Institute," which was a trade-type school for learning about Jim's chosen field, the "ins and outs" of computers.

Shortly after he completed those classes, Jim went to work for NCR starting a career with a giant in cash registers, but NCR was also becoming a giant in the computer industry. After nine years with NCR, Jim was offered a job with Adage Graphics, as not only a computer technician but also troubleshooter. In that position he traveled a lot, which he had a lot of experience doing earlier in his life. Jim even went to Israel twice to set up equipment for the Israeli Air Force. Jim had become one the "best" at his trade with the work ethic he learned from Dad and with the help that Dad had provided when nobody knew what "it" was!

Now Dad was a tough father, and sometimes he was a little bit too hard on his sons. But by the time it got to me, he had softened his approach in raising his boys. Thanks go toward Jim for absorbing all of Dad's blunders and not becoming what Dad was most afraid of: a lazy, lying, thief of a son. Now Mom had those among her lists of things that she would not tolerate. But Dad had a slightly different perspective toward those same things. This was because it was all work related with Dad. Being lazy meant not giving the full effort toward the work it required, while lying meant taking credit for someone else's efforts. Being a thief meant a combination of the first two: too lazy to do the work but wanting to get paid as if they did!

With me, like I earlier noted, Dad had a softer approach. He didn't blame me for having interests aside from work. He didn't call those interests which I had away from work "tom-foolery" or foolish nonsense as he had with Jim. He was able to be a spectator of one of "his boys," me, and my activities outside of work. Dad had even started coming to my high school basketball games.

Dad also had a twenty by twenty concrete slab poured in the back of our lot there in Goddard with a basketball goal and backboard for me to practice shooting! To me, Dad had become a "great" Dad! But Dad was different from many of the other fathers. He didn't want to stand in conspicuous places to watch his sons as they competed in sports. Maybe that was an area that he did not know how to be a Dad in that situation. He did not want to be seen as taking credit for his son's play. Look up: thief, Dad's dictionary. That was not Dad's way! He was in a place where, evidently, he was very uncomfortable. His work had always been where he was very confident and very comfortable. He knew how to work, but he didn't know how to show his boys his love for them. Showing emotions like that was not Dad!

In fact, the day after we lost the State Championship game, Dad handed me a ticket stub for me to keep. It was from "The State Championship game!" He had been there! I think by giving me that and in the way he gave it, alone, just him and me, he was saying he was proud of me! In his own way of course! I never checked the seat number or location. By the time I thought about it, the stub was just a blank stub, all the ink had faded away.

But knowing Dad and his ways, I would put him in the most inconspicuous seat in the arena! Dad could be very invisible to his boys when it was about his boys' achievements. Our younger brothers, Bill and Bob, said that he had taken them to some of the oldest brother Jim's basketball games. Did Dad make his presence at Jim's ball games known to Jim or for that matter to anybody else? No, he did not! How many of Jim's games did Dad go to? Quite a few according to Bill and Bob! Talk about Dad being invisible! That was Dad, my Dad, our Dad!

Just as I treasured that time of growing up in my life, I also treasured those times after Mom and Dad moved out to Nashville, Kansas, as did the other brothers. Those times were like gold when the brothers made that trek to spend special time with them. The wild and competitive horseshoe matches with Dad being one of the competitors will always be fond memories to each of us. Dad with his proud and distinctive walk to the other end after he had thrown a "ringer" was one of those delightful memories! Those times can't be bought! They can be only lived in memories by those who were there, of those happy times!

Later on, as time passed and his hard way of life had caught up to him, Dad was only able to be a spectator of "his boys" activities. He was unable to be a participant in those events. Often Dad and Mom would stop by our job. Dad would pick up bent nails and tell whichever of "his boys" closest to him, "You do know you can straighten these and still use them." It was straight out of the depression years he had lived through! Jim would move back from California in the 1980s. The four brothers still in Kansas did a lot of things together in the 1970s and 1980s, even working in residential home construction together! Those four brothers also played slow pitch softball together, with us winning many more games than we lost. That was not surprising as we played just like we worked hard! We also carried our love for "pitching horseshoes" from the side yard of Dad and Mom's house in Nashville to our softball games, and at every chance between those games, we "pitched shoes." Mom and Dad watched us play in many of those soft ball games and the horseshoe pitching tournaments between games.

Dad would always have his famous line ready to tell his boys, "You're burning daylight," which always meant "You could be out working instead of 'playing'," but then he would laugh after saying it. He even used that "line" whenever we drove out to visit Mom and him, but he would always chuckle after saying his "famous line" then also. Jim would even join us later on after moving back from California. Jim and his family bought a house that the Knowles Boys had built in Cheney, Kansas, for them.

The five "Knowles boys" would be together once more! The family, all seven of us, would spend many more moments, together! Laughing at things that before had been serious stuff to Dad and to all of us!

The vagabond family, which had many tough times early on, had finally found a home. At first it was thought to be Goddard, but that is just a place, a house with its address numbers on its front. We finally figured out that a home really isn't just a bunch of numbers on the front of it, but it is a feeling of belonging that comes when a family shares the love it has for its members. It isn't a place at all, but a feeling of belonging!

Back row, left to right—Bill, Bob, Moochie, Jim, and Chuck
Front row, left to right—Dad and Mom

# Growing Up in the Fifties in a Small Midwestern Town

# Chapter 1

## Games Kids Played

Kids today have everything from five hundred channels on TV to the Internet. From twenty-four-hour *SportsCenter* to televised games in every possible sport that is played. From electronic games played on the Internet to games that can be played on your phone, the games are endless. But we hear it every day, from our kids and from our grandkids, "but there's nothing to do!" Sometimes having everything means having nothing. A normal day in the summer of the 1950s was spent getting out of the house and out of Mom's hair. Playing real games with other neighborhood kids, not just playing games with computer-generated images!

Games like "work-up" where one kid batted while another kid pitched and all the other kids played in the field trying to get the batter out. When the batter got put out, then the kid who pitched became the batter, and every kid 'moved up': first base to pitcher, second base to first base, and so on. After the batter is put out, he moves to right field and starts his "working up" all over again. If you have extra players, then they become the next batters, and if the previous batter reaches a base, he becomes a runner. When any out is made, that player becomes the right fielder, and that includes any base runner also. One great thing about kids playing games is that the rules can be changed to fit the situation as long as it is not in the middle of the game.

The list of games can be endless with just a ball and a bat and an active imagination! I remember one game we called "500." The game where a ball caught in the air got a hundred points. And balls caught that bounced got other points. Like a one hopper got seventy-five points, a two hopper got fifty and so forth, until you got to five hundred and started over. The only change: the winner gets to bat!

Basketball can have games with just a basketball. And if you have a goal in your driveway, the list of games gets bigger! If you have an outdoor court, basketball can have competitive one-on-one all the way to real five on five. "Horse" is a great game, and kids get a lesson in how to spell at the same time! All the games we played growing up in the 1950s just took a little imagination and couple of kids.

Sure we had threats from "older kids," bullies and such, but it seemed they disappeared when the younger kids banded together as a group. We also had the protection of older brothers if it went beyond the normal threat. I had two older brothers, so nobody even tried to threaten me or any of our group on Spruce Street. I'm also sure we had sick nutjobs like the ones mothers fear today, but kids in our little town basically played together as a group. If there were any of those types, they never threatened us. The older kids looked out for the younger ones, and no reports made the news in our little town. The kids in our little town learned the value of friendship, and it locked the kids together in a protective web.

The mothers, especially on Spruce Street, would come out on their porches and yell, "Lunch is ready, kids!" This call would cause all the kids to drop everything and run home! And I don't remember any of our "stuff" being stolen while we ate lunch.

I have close friendships, over sixty years in the making, and the time is still being added to those friendships today! This is an area that I worry about today as we become less about learning to interact with each other and more about interacting with electronic games that kids and adults play all ALONE. We seem to be building a society of loners. Look around at all the finely built neighborhoods. How many people even know who lives next door? Part of the glue that held neighborhoods and communities together were the young kids and their play! In the 1950s, it was the interaction of kids playing with the other kids of their neighborhoods that created the glue. Neighbors knew other neighbors because of kids starting the chance to meet through their play! Yes, keeping the kids close by and in the house playing video games maybe a way to protect them, but, to me, it is at a terrible price.

What are the kids of today learning? Are they learning about the value of a life in simulated situations on a video screen? Do we want our kids thinking that a life is just a simulated man or woman on the screen there only an instant until it can be eliminated by pushing a button on the mouse of the computer? Are we stupid enough to not know what we are creating? WE are creating a society of our own worst fears! In the mass murders of today, the description of the murderer much of the time contains: "He was a loner; he didn't have many friends; he stayed by himself most of his time!" In the 1950s we learned so much more about the real important things in life! Like the value of having others as friends, real, not computer-generated! Always remember the song by "Three Dog Night" . . . "One" . . . "One is the loneliest number." Okay, I'm off my soapbox. How about we go FISHING! Get the poles, seine, and gunny sacks. Seine and gunny sacks?

Our fishing expeditions usually took place in the afternoon. One of those was a trip to a creek southeast of Garden Plain. It was a creek where Rick McKay said he had caught a ten-pound catfish. It was, "had caught," as he had caught it without Chuck and I to witness it. Rick was a straight shooter that never lied, but a ten-pound catfish would have to be an exaggeration. Knowing that we wouldn't believe him, Rick brought the fish with him. There it was right in front of us, and he handed Chuck his scale. Yep, ten-pounder, as Chuck checked the scale and verified the weight. Yep, a ten-pound yellow "cat" in fisherman language!

Rick was tall, but not a "tall tale-teller," Rick was in our oldest brother's Jim's class, but Rick and Chuck shared the same "love," fishing. When they would talk to each other, they could finish each other's sentences before the other finished saying it. Their topic was always about one thing, fishing! Rick had returned, the "day of the yellow catfish," to get a few things, a seine and some gunny sacks.

Rick hadn't finished his sentence before Chuck blurted out, "You want us to come and help you seine that creek?" After seeing the catfish, Chuck wanted nothing more than see if another was laying in that creek just waiting for him to catch it.

Chuck didn't even wait for Rick to answer as he was already sprinting for the door to call out to Mom. "Steve and I are going fishing with Rick!" I didn't hear Mom's answer, and I doubt Chuck did either. We went by Rick's house grabbing the seine, and we were off with Rick leading the way. We took the ten-pound catfish and put him in a tank at Rick's house.

The trip to the creek was around four miles as it seemed like the second bridge where Chuck and I fished a lot was about half way. I know I didn't know how far it was, and I don't think Chuck did either. We did know it was going to be an adventure. All of our journeys with Rick were THAT!

Now Rick knew how to pace himself on long walks as he walked everywhere he went, but he was about a foot taller than Chuck, and with his long strides Chuck had to walk really fast to keep up. I had to trot to keep up with them. I was really tired when we got to the creek. Rick and Chuck started seining the creek as I rested on the bank. Rick had left the gunny sacks on the bank. I had never seined before; Rick threw a couple of fish up on the bank and told me to "bag em." Well, I'm not a rocket scientist, but I figured out what the gunny sacks were for; they were the bags I was to put the fish in!

After a while, Rick decided we had enough fish, and he and Chuck climbed out of the creek. Many of the fish were "channel cat," and no fish was as big as the yellow cat Rick had caught earlier, but we had a lot of fish! With the fish all bagged and separated into the gunny sacks, we started our long walk back. We had tied the filled gunny sacks to the belt loops of our jeans. Each of us had two gunny sacks.

That's when we found out the only wrong decision that we had ever seen Rick make. The fish had very sharp fins, especially the channel cats! With every step we would make, the sharp fins coming from the sides of the channel cats would stab us in the leg through our jeans. Those fins would also cut through the gunny sacks. Soon, we had fish falling out of the gunny sacks. At first I picked them up and put them back into the gunny sacks, but after a while I started leaving them where they lay after they fell out through the ever-widening holes in the sacks. By the time we could see Goddard in the distance, what was left of my gunny sacks held not a fish. I don't believe Chuck's had any either. But that field must have been well fertilized (old Indian way to fertilize); it did look a lot greener the next year!

Most of the way back, I just looked down at the ground in order to keep going as I was not sure I could make it home. Now Rick, Chuck, and I had jeans, but those fins had to be doing some damage to our legs through those jeans. We would soon find out the damage those fins did! Well, it turned out to be not as bad as I thought, but it sure hurt when those fins stuck us. Lesson learned: always wear double or triple layers of jeans when going fishing with Rick!

We never went back to that creek southeast of Garden Plain. We heard that it was kind of "fished out." I didn't bother adding my thoughts to anybody of why it was "fished out!" But we did visit the creek at what we called the second bridge: two lakes with a creek that connected the two of them. We never knew what adventure we would find there, but from blue racer snakes to big snapping turtles, we always seem to find something there. We even found, in the rocks put around the supports of the railroad trestle, interesting fossils that showed life from long ago! I took some of them home for "show and tell" in school. Anybody remember "show and tell" from grade school?

## Chapter 2

# Dizzy and Pee Wee, Bike Races, Pole Vaulting, Ping Pong, and Whiffle Ball

Although fishing took some of our time, other things were a part of our lives, too. Things like *The Game of the Week* with Dizzy Dean and Pee Wee Reese. Once a week, we got to see a major league game, and just about every kid who played baseball watched it every week. That game was on every Saturday and was the only game on TV! But later on, a game on Sunday would be added. Our major league baseball doubled with that happening!

In fact there was no NFL on TV during the fall months nor NBA during the winter months either! We also had very little TV coverage of college basketball or college football, so what did we do? We participated in everything. We usually had about a month of practice before our youth league baseball started. We usually played two league baseball games a week. And we usually had at least one practice a week after league started. So little league baseball kept us pretty busy. Now everybody knows how important little league baseball was to Moochie. The movie was after all called *Moochie of the Little League* . . . Oops, that was Kevin not Steve . . . AKA Moochie of Goddard! How about we get our bikes and have BIKE RACES?

During the summer we raced our bikes on a half-mile course around the two blocks of Walnut and Spruce. That's another thing about small Kansas towns in the 1950s, very little car traffic, so bike races can be held. Some days we upped the distance to one mile which would mean two laps around the double block of Spruce and Walnut. We would have kids every so often to warn riders of possible danger, like moving cars! Well, the distance we called our races was not officially verified, but that was what it seemed like! Tired? How about some POLE VAULTING? Get the pole and the shovels! Shovels?

Many kids on Spruce Street fell in love with pole vaulting. It started with us using cane poles that we got from carpet installers, as the carpet always had a cane pole at the center of the rolls of carpet. Later we used the aluminum pole bought from a sporting goods store by our oldest brother, Jim, after his first journey into the world of work! We would build a pole chute for the pole to go into, and we dug the dirt by hand that we landed in. By turning the dirt over and re-digging it after a couple of jumps, it may not have been OSHA approved, but nobody broke any bones among our group of kids who pole vaulted. The only difference between our vaulting pits and the school's was the sand that was in the school's pits. There were not airbags to land in at that time. One of the first things we learned in pole vaulting was how to fall. Another term for that is "learning how to land," but it is a fall, a hopefully controlled one but a fall. How about a little "PING PONG? Get the paddles and your running shoes on! Running shoes?

We also played a lot of table tennis (ping pong), which took some preparation. We started with a garage that we cleaned out enough to have a sixteen by twelve foot area in the center of a garage. So we needed a two-car garage. The only two-car garage we had available was the Voge's. I wonder if Roger's Dad ever figured out why his garage was always pretty clean, especially in the middle of it. Like maybe about a twelve by sixteen foot area! We would then build a set of saw horses, and we, or a kindly father or mother (it seemed like everyone in our neighborhood wanted to keep us busy doing something for some reason), would provide, or buy, a four by eight sheet of ¾-inch plywood to be the top of the table (table tennis) (mr). A small can of paint to put a stripe down the middle and a set of four paddles, a net, and some ping pong balls, and then you could hear somebody say the "whose serve is it?" Kind of like the sound of "start your engines" at the beginning of the Indianapolis 500! So when it was raining or the sun was "just too hot" or just because we wanted to, we played "ping pong!" Singles, doubles, mixed doubles, boy versus girl, we had every combination of matches.

We even had a game we called "around the horn" which is a game that can only be described by using the letters A, B, C, and D for the four players. Players A and B are on one end, and players C and D are on the other end. A serves to D, and then the game changes, as A runs to the other end to replace D, as D hits the ball to B. D then runs to the other end to replace B, while B hits the ball to C. B runs around the table to replace C, as C hits the ball to D. C runs to the other end to replace D, as D hits the ball to A, and so on. GOT THAT, so far? This hitting and running continue until a player misses the table or hits into the net or does not get to the ball. That player is eliminated, and the other three then start a frantic chase of hitting and running until another player gets eliminated. Then the scoring round starts with the two players left playing for the point. The game's winner is the player who gets to whatever number decided at the beginning. This game combines speed with agility for those who keep track of the worth of an activity. Does anybody need an illustration?

1.) A serves to D, then runs to the other end of the table. B slides over to cover the end A left.

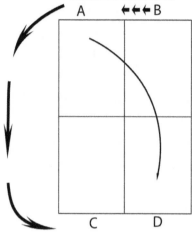

2.) D returns to B, then runs to the other end of the table. C slides over to cover the end D left.

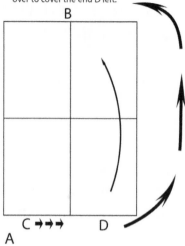

3.) B returns to C, then runs to the other end of the table. D slides over to cover the end B left.

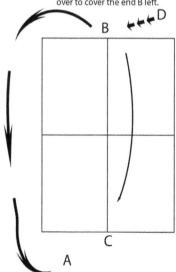

4.) C returns to D, then runs to the other end of the table. A slides over to cover the end C left.

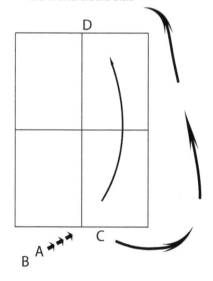

5.) D returns to A, then runs to the other end of the table. C slides over to cover the end D left.

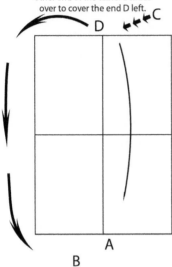

6.) A returns to C, then runs to the other end of the table. B slides over to cover the end A left.

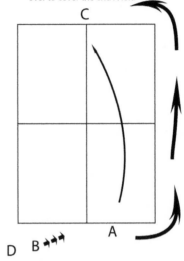

7.) C returns to B, then runs to the other end of the table. A slides over to cover the end C left.

8.) B returns to A, then runs to the other end of the table. D slides over to cover the end B left.

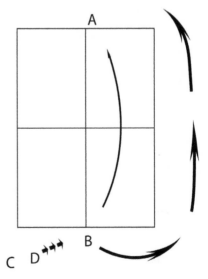

Confused? Well it was a confusing game with a lot of running mixed in!

After the sun goes down, and the activity calms down, we brought out the transistor radios and tried to get our favorite team's game on. If it was cold (spring or fall), we would go inside and listen to the game on the big house radio. But most of the time, in the summer, we listened to the game on our small transistor radios. Sometimes you had to "aim it" just right, but we were inventive; there wasn't much that we couldn't do! How about some WHIFFLE BALL? Get the mower and the tape. Mower? Tape?

Yes, we had whiffle ball games with plastic balls and plastic bats. After a few of those games, the plastic balls would get cracked, so we take tape and wrap the ball up tight. This led to the plastic bats getting bent and useless to hit the taped up balls. So we taped the bats! Show us a problem, and we would come up with a solution! There were a couple of empty lots across the street, so those became our "whiffle ball diamond." We mowed the infield and left the outfield un-mowed except for a strip that circled the outside perimeter of the field. Roger's Dad said we mowed our "whiffle ball diamond" more than his yard! But we had to as the mowing was part of the rules we played under. Anything hit over that strip that we mowed for the perimeter was a home run! We even built a backstop with chicken wire and "scrap wood" as the taped up balls could now fly into the street. As I noted before, we were inventive, and there was nothing that we couldn't do!

Of our players, at that time, I was the oldest, Roger Voge was the second oldest, with next three being the same age, my brothers, Bob, Bill, and a neighbor kid, who was Roger's younger brother, Sid Voge. The youngest was Tim Voge, obviously Roger and Sid's younger brother. So the whole setup was two sets of brothers. Roger, Tim, and I formed one team. Bill, Bob, and Sid were the other team. Everybody in that group of six had a part in the construction of the field. I don't remember much about the games, but the making of the diamond and the adapting of the changing condition of the ball and bat illustrate how kids from that time period "got up and dusted themselves off and said," "Okay now what do we do!" And did it!

An interesting side note, I considered growing up in Goddard as pretty much normal growing up but the five Knowles boys, Jim, Chuck, Steve (Moochie), Bill, and Bob, (no girls) were matched by the five Voge boys, Roger, Sid, Timmy, Tad, and Donny, (no girls) (mr). The only thing that was ever between one set of brothers (the Knowles boys) to the other set of brothers (the Voge boys) was Spruce Street. The Knowles boys grew up directly across Spruce Street from the Voge boys, NOT very normal AT ALL.

# Chapter 3

## Now What? Monopoly, Baseball Box and Make-Believe

There were many other games we played in the summers. It all depended on our imagination as to how the game was played. The old-time favorite "tag" was played with a football as being the instrument of the tag. Swing long jump was obviously jumping out of a swing at the highest point and wherever the landing point was where the jumper stayed until somebody beat it. If one of the Spruce Street moms would have seen us jumping out of the swings, she would have become "unglued" and put an end to our game.

Cold weather made us bring out board games like monopoly, scrabble, clue, and checkers. A monopoly game could last for hours, so we learned how to shorten it by dividing the properties at the start of the game. We also played some card games, like poker, but with many wild cards, like baseball with 3s, 9s, and one-eyed jacks or Dr. Pepper with 2s, 10s, and 4s. In other card games, we would make up rules out of our imagination.

We did have "pinball machines" at some places, but I didn't want to spend my hard-earned money like that. No way was I going to beg Dad for "pinball money" as that would have got me a slap to my head or worse. If I was going to play "pinball" I would have to make it, myself.

So that is what I set out to do. First I needed to build a frame. I measured and cut four, one by fours. Two of them three feet, the other two, thirty-four and a half inches long. I wanted a box exactly three feet by three feet outside dimensions. I nailed the box together with the three-foot boards over the thirty-four and a half boards. I then secured a three foot by three foot piece of cardboard to the bottom of the frame. I had drawn a baseball diamond on it with a one-foot square to indicate the infield.

Where every player played, I wrote the position, and in front of that I cut a slot to hold a baseball card. In front of that I cut a hole; this would be for the marbles to drop through and that would be an out. In the outfield, I put slots for the baseball cards with the holes in front of those cards. Those would be fly ball outs. Around the outfield, near the outside two 1 by 4s, it was called "in fair ground" hits if it finds a hole for hits. For those I cut holes and had double holes twice and triple and home run holes once each. But the holes were more like large slots. I then put a nail into a dowel of about three inches. This would be the bat. I put the nail through a hole on home plate. This is to spin the nail in the fingers "to bat." I then nailed four three-foot boards for the legs to hold up the box. I draped a gunny sack under and secured it to the box. This was to catch the marbles used for the balls. So with that completed all I needed was another kid to be my opponent. Just like in major league baseball, it takes two teams to play ball!

Later, I had to "procure" a piece of plywood to be the "floor of the field" as with the number of holes and slots made the cardboard too weak! This brought another tool into the making, a jigsaw. The pitcher's card also had to be replaced a couple of times each game as it took a lot of hits "up the middle!" Just like major league baseball, you need a bullpen!

As we played, we found other rules needed to be made, like balls that do not find a hole or slot were called a foul ball. Sometimes the players' card would tilt back and the ball (marble) would become airborne. Those would be outs, as they did hit a card.

Another game we played only had our imagination. We called it "make-believe." One kid would start a story, usually an adventure story, and then the second kid would add to that. Then a third kid would add to the story. It seemed like each would have something that they would be interested in at that time. If it was "monsters," then we would be fighting monsters. If it was baseball, then we would win the game with home runs. Sometimes, it seemed, one interest would battle the other interest for control of the story. Something like "Willie Mays" fights "Godzilla" makes one wonder if a movie producer was hiding in the weeds listening! I wonder if today's kids have anything close to "make-believe."

Now, we might have said "but there's nothing to do," but around Mom that would bring Mom's reply, "Get a book and read!" Much of the time our activities would start with the building of the game. Or the getting of what we needed in the game. Then we would start the games. Whether it was the table tennis (ping pong) setup . . . We made it! Whether it was the pole vaulting poles and pits . . . We made it happen! Or the making of the box to compete against each other in an inventive form of "pin ball baseball!" We invented and made it! Or in other games we made the rules as we went along! And on top of all those activities, we did a lot of READING also! As sometimes, we did let it slip out . . . "But there's nothing to do!" But if the truth were to be known . . . We did like all those adventures other kids had in those stories! Many times we would use those stories to start our own "make-believe" stories.

Okay, we did have that box in the living room, what was that called . . . oh yeah . . . TV. Lots of great westerns . . . *The Lone Ranger* . . . *Wyatt Earp* . . . *Wanted Dead or Alive* . . . *Gunsmoke* . . . *Have Gun—Will Travel* . . . *Wells Fargo* . . . *Death Valley Days* . . . *Roy Rogers* . . . *Gene Autry*. There was the beginning of game shows . . . *I've Got a Secret* . . . *What's My Line?* Sitcoms also . . . *Ozzie and Harriet* . . . *I Love Lucy* . . . *Honeymooners*. Some funny comedians . . . *Burns and Allen*. And variety shows like *Ed Sullivan* . . . But we also got to see the beginning of superheroes on TV like "look, up in the sky, is it a bird, is it a plane, no it's Superman!" But when Dad was home, it was his choice, not ours! And of course *The Friday Night Fights* were at the top of Dad's list of choices.

So we did have that new and wonderful television to watch. But during the day, it was filled with soap operas like *Days of Our Lives* and local TV shows like *House Party*.

The whole new "it thing," the television, and its visionaries were stumbling around looking for the next new craze that would bring in viewers. Most of the "daytime" stuff wasn't anything we would skip any of our other exciting things we wanted to do! Except of course the *World Series*, and we kids would watch every moment of it. Believe it or not, baseball was exciting back then! Then in 1955 came Walt Disney's *The Mickey Mouse Club* show, and we had our own show! It also was the cause of the birth of Moochie, my alter ego? All of us boys fell hopelessly in love with Annette. And the TV industry found out that the under eighteen group was also a viable market. So TV started focusing on the kids, and their made-for-kids shows took away our need for using our imagination; we had television!

The TV screen was a huge 13 inches, and there were also great "new words" to describe the picture quality like "snowy," blurry, and fuzzy. Many times the picture would "roll," which was called the "vertical hold" messing up. Or it would shrink in from the side, which was called the "horizontal hold" messing up. If you are over sixty years old, do you remember the intro to *The Outer Limits* . . . It starts with the test pattern . . . Then the "Control" voice starts . . . "There is nothing wrong with your television . . . Do not attempt to adjust the picture . . . We are now in control of the transmission . . . We control the horizontal and the vertical . . . We can deluge you with a thousand channels . . . or expand one single image to crystal clarity and beyond . . . We can shape your vision to anything our imagination can conceive . . . For the next hour, we will control all that you see or hear." This early television show "intro" illustrated all the realities of the early TV sets.

These early problems of, basically, a new era in technology actually caused a whole new industry to be created. The television repair industry, and the stars of it, the TV repairmen! In this instance advances in technology created a new industry, but that industry was also "a sign of the times!" Technology could also be blamed for that industry's downfall into the dust pan of history. "A sign of the times" is also in many more types of industry as new advances sweep many more industries into that dust pan. The march of technology moves on, but what about its effect on our society? What about the effects of it on our children? Did we teach them how to live in this new world we've created? I wonder, did we?

Looking back to those times, it might have been TV that started the era of creating loners. The TV, plus all the other technology, may have become the free babysitter in many houses. Adding to that, a mother's natural fear of letting her kids out of her sight where so many bad things could happen to them. That fear was increased by the need of the media constantly reinforcing that fear because of the need to have more and more gruesome news stories. Later our "advanced society" would advance into computers, and the "loner" became the norm of the society we created, not the exception.

TV was also only in "black and white" in the 1950s. The technology of that would change in the 1960s with the advent of color television. The march of technology took another step.

We cannot bring the 1950s back, but we should know what has evolved from that era. We could learn the lessons that have been taught to us since those "boring" days of the 1950s!

# Mike and Moochie

# *Chapter 1*

This may not make sense unless the reader understands the rules of Moochie-isms. So study up on thinking Moochie and speaking Moochie and most importantly understanding Moochie. "I" and "me" are really Moochie, or Moochie's alter egos. "My" and "mine" are Moochie talking ownership. Moochie talking to Moochie is third person Moochie! GOT THAT, So far?

There were many Mikes among my childhood friends: Mike Herndon and Micol Preboth, just to name two. But early on, it was Mike Teter who was one of my closest friends. We are still good friends even after sixty plus years of knowing each other! In fact, Mike was my "technical" advisor on this story (keeping me straight on all the facts, as this was fifty years ago!)

My Mom used to laugh at the Mike and Moochie (my) relationship and all the twists and turns it would make. Now Mike had both legs amputated between the third and fourth grade and started grade school at Goddard in the middle of the fourth grade. Mike and another classmate, Rita, transferred from Christ the King grade school that year. I didn't know Mike prior to that time, obviously! But when I did, we became "good buddies." Sorry Rita, too busy, let's get back, no not *Back to the Future* sorry to another Mike, Michael J. Fox, but getting back to Mike and Moochie!

My Mom would always laugh at my complaints about Mike. Like I would grow to be taller than Mike, and then he would get a new set of prosthetics and be taller than me! Sometimes Mike would lose his balance and fall, and I would help him get up. But Mike would get that look on his face that said loudly "I DON'T NEED ANY HELP!" although he never said it with words! I told Mom about that, and she would laugh and say, "You just keep helping him up, anyway."

You see Mike was very, very independent, in fact if you helped Mike, it seemed like he was doing you a favor by letting you help him. I think his Dad was very instrumental in raising Mike so he would develop that attitude! That might have been why Mike was my Mom's favorite of all my friends! Understanding Mike is a lot like understanding Moochie!

Grade school came and went, but it was in junior high and later high school where Mike and Moochie (me) developed our love for "rock and roll" music. We spent a lot of time in high school competing against one another in our knowledge of "rock and roll." When cars entered our lives, a couple of things changed, but not our common love of "rock and roll."

But having it "blasting out" from our car's radio at almost anywhere (except church, of course) we went made us, in our minds, cool! We also found "our" "rock and roll" station, not only on the "dial," it was KLEO 1480, but we found the actual station! Actually, I think it was Mike who found it! It was in the middle of a field with a small building being the station and the radio tower that sent out the sound of "rock and roll" to the world!

Whenever we wanted to visit "our Mecca of rock and roll" now we could go to where it was! Mike, Jim Hake, (another classmate and friend), and Moochie (me) made that trip many times! The disc jockeys who "spun" the discs were known as "Uncle Harvey" and "Johnny Midnight." Each time we went to "our Mecca of our rock and roll," the same play would start, and it was just like the scene from *American Graffiti*

Johnny or Uncle Harvey would always ask, "What high school are you kids from?" To which we would answer loudly, "GODDARD HIGH!" Then whoever disc jockey was on the mic would say, "Got a bunch of kids here from Goddard High and what would you kids like to hear tonight!" Actually there were only three of us so we would "loudly" YELL out our answer in order to make it seem like a bunch of kids. And in a couple of seconds the disc would be spinning.

Then our choice would be "blasting out" for all of the world (or at least the part that was important to us) to hear! The choice had to be good or that world of kids as far as that tower could send it would know that Goddard High was a bunch of losers. But if it was a good choice, Goddard High would be "a group of really COOL KIDS!" That was a lot of pressure, but we, most of time it was Mike's choice, but Jim, and I (Moochie), were with Mike so it was "we could handle it!" We knew all the songs, all the titles, and all the artists, of our music, rock and roll!

With the driving of our cars came the burden of having to put gas in them.

Having "wheels" was a very important part of growing up, and "in the 1960s" it meant a girl in the seat beside you and "rock and roll" blasting out from the car's radio. It meant, for most of us, a reason to have a job! Most of us did find jobs, or at least part-time jobs!

My first real job was on a trash truck. I think I was fourteen, and I made $1 an hour! At least I (Moochie) didn't have to wear a silly uniform, and I did become a lot stronger by lifting those barrels full of trash. At fifteen, I (Moochie) was offered a job with a neighbor's roofing company, (Voge Brothers), and I (Moochie) made $1.50 an hour when we roofed peoples' houses and $2.00 an hour when we worked on commercial roofs that were done with "hot tar." Hot tar was more dangerous as I (Moochie) found out later. My (Moochie's) job on the "residential homes" was to carry 90-lb bundles of shingles from the truck to the roof.

Sometimes the truck couldn't get close enough to use the lift, and I (Moochie) would have to carry the shingles however far the distance was from the house and then up a ladder and on to the roof. "When this old world starts getting me down . . . And people are just too much for me to face . . . I climb way up to the top of the stairs . . . And all my cares just drift right into space . . . On the roof, it's peaceful as it can be . . . And there the world below can't bother me." Oops got tied up to the Drifters *Up on the Roof* for a moment. Sometimes the mind really wanders when doing monotonous work.

Where was I, oh yeah . . . I had to stay ahead of the neighbor, Dale Voge, and his brother, Clarence, in carrying the shingles on to the roof at least as fast as those two could roof. And those two were said to be the fastest roofers in the business! I believed that reputation, because they averaged three of the standard houses of that time a day! They told me their record for the most squares put on in a day was seventy-nine for just the two of them! I believed them because they came close to that record in some of those days during the summers that I worked for their roofing company. There is one question that I wished I had asked at that time, "Who got forty and who got thirty-nine?" That was, and still is, an incredible number!

There were other benefits besides making enough money to put gas in our cars. Just carrying 90-lb bundles of shingles from the bed of a lift truck has a major effect on a young body. When the lift truck couldn't get close enough to the house to use the lift, I had a problem. In each square of shingles are three bundles each of which weigh 90 lbs. An average house would take around twenty-three to twenty-six squares of shingles. That comes to sixty-nine to seventy-eight 90-lb bundles I would have to carry. And that would be for just one of the houses we were going to roof that day! My thoughts were more like a prayer; please oh please, let us get close enough on the next house to use the lift! I knew I was going to be a "tired puppy" at the end of the day!

As I had to carry all of the 90-lb bundles, from the truck to the house, up a ladder on to the roof . . . a song started running through my head…"from the locker to the blanket, from the blanket to the shore, from the shore to the water . . . Stick around we'll tell you more!" . . . oops, I got lost in Brian Hyland's *Itsy Bitsy, Teenie Weenie Yellow Polka-dot Bikini*, where were we? Oh yeah . . . that extra carrying did even more to build a young body's strength! It had a major effect on strengthening my legs. And once again it's very hard to carry 90-lb bundles without the mind starting to wander all over the place.

But I will say that they would give me breaks. They would leave the last three shingles on each row for me to rest while doing them. Wow, thanks, Clarence and Dale, you are too kind! They said it was to teach me how to roof! But I knew better. That was like what roofing with the best means, a break is sitting and doing the installing of the shingles on the roof! But it did make my legs a lot stronger; this would help me in what I wanted to prove my senior year in basketball.

I had gone out for basketball every year from junior high and through my sophomore year. But I decided to "sit" out my junior year from playing basketball for the high school team. Being very short compared to the others on the team, none of coaches would ever play me anyway, so playing for the varsity was a waste of time! So I stopped trying to play for the varsity team, but not from playing basketball. I loved basketball!

I played with the Alumni team. Every year during the Christmas break, the Alumni played the high school varsity in a basketball game. I had a lot of friends on both teams, and the head coach was in his first year at Goddard, so the fix was on! The Alumni knew how much I wanted to prove to the "powers that be" (the new coaching staff): that I could play! After the Alumni made me look like the star of the Alumni team, it seemed my friends on the high school team also got in the conspiracy as every shot I took was wide open.

I ended up scoring about twenty-five points and got what I wanted to prove and more! The head coach of our high school team asked me after the game, "What are you doing playing for the Alumni? Aren't you still in high school?" I replied "Yes, but I never got to play." He replied, "If you come out next year, I guarantee you'll play!" I wasn't as good as everybody made me look that day, but I think I deserved to start, and the coach started me every game that I could play!

I said the coach started me every game that I COULD because early in the year I suffered a head injury in the game against Anthony. I probably had a concussion from being knocked down by Anthony's center Cliff Elliott and landed on by Jerry Cox, Anthony's big forward. Anthony played a "zone defense," so we played our "zone offense" in which I played on the baseline. I had received a pass on the baseline, and I faked a shot which Jerry Cox bit on and jumped up to block my shot. He ended up flying by me so I took a couple of dribbles to get a little closer, and I shot the ball. Big Cliff (6'7") blocked my attempt but knocked me down, and he also went down. Big Jerry (6'5"), who had first blown by me on his attempt to block my shot, which was a fake, had recovered. In fact, he was hustling to get back into the play. But he tripped on the mass of bodies and landed on top of me.

The force of big Jerry's fall drove the back of my head into the floor. It caused me to have a case of double vision!

In any type of calamity, I always tried to find something positive. In this case, it was that Jerry's twin, big John Cox, didn't join the bodies on the floor! Big John Cox was also 6'5" and 240 lb, and with all three of them in the pile, it might have caused a "death count" instead of "injury count" and most likely a sagging floor. After all of the body parts were counted and the floor was ruled safe, play resumed. After Steeby made a couple passes to me where I tried to catch the wrong ball, coach took me out. Out for not only the rest of that game, but he didn't play me in our next game either!

The next game was against Garden Plain. I had a lot of buddies on that team that I played with in summer baseball! I missed that game, but my double vision cleared up. I was back to starting after that pause in my basketball career. I know I should have told coach of my vision problem, but this was the only season I could play for Goddard.

I figured that playing that season was the most important thing in my life, so I just toughed it out! I was starting, and I wasn't going to let another doctor end my basketball season! One had taken away my football seasons already! By the way, we lost the game to Garden Plain as Bobby Renner (shortstop and pitcher) scored twenty-two points and Alan Schauf (first base) scored sixteen. It was our first loss that year. I was listed as DNP (did not play).

I did have something that was not shown in that Alumni/Varsity game over that Christmas break the year before. An ability to jump incredibly high due to not only my working in the summers carrying 90-lb bundles up ladders but also by something inherent in my family. My oldest brother, Jim, had always jumped center at the start of his games during his high school career.

He was three inches taller than I, but he also played on a team that had two players on the starting five who were about a half a foot taller than Jim! So my ability to jump was "in my blood" as they used to say. The summers spent carrying heavy bundles took my inherent ability to jump to a new level. It was around that ability that I based my contribution to the basketball team. I may not have been able to shoot, but I could really jump!

I developed some tricks to get into "jump ball" situations with members of the other team. Although I told my teammates that it was just my desire to get an "up close" look at our cheerleaders' legs; and they did have beautiful legs, but the diving on the floor was, in reality, the final act of one of my tricks toward the one who was "my man" to guard on the other team. I figured with every dribble he made that the ball was up for grabs as soon as it left his hand and until it was back in his hand again. My trick was to time my attack on that time period that the ball was up for "grabs" and get to where it was by diving on the floor. Many times it became a jump ball because both of us ended up on the floor wrestling to get control of the ball. Another trick I used was as I ran back to play defense, I watched the other opposing players to see how aware they were of me.

Most of the time, the opposing players' attention was on the man who was guarding them, not on me. A quick attack from me was sometimes effective in either a steal or a tie-up, and even if it was not successful, it still made them tentative in their play. I always figured a jump ball was "our" ball as my being short would give the illusion to the other team that they should control the tip of the jump ball, very easily. But things are not always what they appear to be. The jump ball was my territory, and it had become one of our team's weapons to win the games. That was, and had been, a very successful tactic for us all year. In fact, early in the year during a practice, Coach Tillett wanted to have a situation where we knew we were going to lose a jump ball. He chose me to be our team's jumper and 6'1" Kenny Deforest to be the opposing team's jumper. After three times where I easily controlled the tip, he told us to switch our shirts so I would be the opposing team's jumper.

In the Tournament of Champions, at Dodge City, against Shawnee Mission East, I had forced a jump ball by tying up their 6'5" center. In most cases a man with 8+ inches on the shorter man will always win the tip, but many times those taller players don't even really try against a player that much shorter! That is sometimes all I needed to control the tip, overconfidence! The "Man Friday" who was appointed to our team as "chaperone" said, "This won't be fair," to which our injured starter (Mike Herndon) replied, "Yep, we're about to score!" And we did!

Steeby motioned with his eyes which side he wanted me to tip it to, and the shocked "Man Friday" (who relayed this to me) and SM East found out what other teams experienced that year! Now against some really tall players, I sometimes did a little "bending" of the rules by quick jumping, but I never got called for that all year! I did that against that center that day! Most "really" big players are slow to jump, and I had to start my jump as soon as the referee tossed the ball. I guess it was legal as it was never called against me! It was just another trick in my bag!

Another one of my tricks was because of my unusually large hands, for my size. I could "palm" a ball; I used that to sometimes move the ball 6" to 8" at the top of my dribble, with my hand still on top of the ball, and I was never, ever called for palming. Actually, it wasn't palming the ball but double dribble as I had held the ball with my larger than normal hands. That was good for a hesitation in my dribble to keep my man from timing my dribble as I did him.

I used those tricks and my unusual jumping ability all year as it was really my main contribution to the team. Everybody on the team had a role, and that was mine. I did have games that I scored an unusually high amount, for me, but those games were exactly that, unusual! Against Valley Center, the number one ranked team in the state, I scored twelve points. Including four baskets in the first half propelling, according to the newspaper, "Goddard to a first half lead!" Unfortunately, it also called me Rod Knowles; I was like Rodney Dangerfield, "I just can't get any respect!" Unfortunately, I did lose a jump ball in the last game of the season. I found out in the State Championship game that Kenny Wiens of Inman could also jump very well, and he was six inches taller!

When I was able to tie him up, he wasn't taking my size to get overconfident as many others had done; he controlled that jump ball, and for the first time that year I lost a jump ball. My loss of that tip wasn't pointed out in the paper; the really big reason pointed out was that our top scorer Steeby was playing with one eye almost completely swollen shut, but to me it was also my failure to do what I had done all year. It was, after all, a team game, and everybody has to do their part. Doug Duncan and his brother, Gary, contributed by rebounding and hitting timely shots; Mike Herndon actually led us by scoring eighteen points in the championship game, but I failed in contributing my specialty! I really took the loss hard.

Of course the positioning of our main offensive weapon (Steeby) on the offensive side of the circle might have given away our team's belief that we were going to win that tip against Wiens. Or it could have been our first possession where Doug and I switched positions as Doug took their center out of the middle. Leaving me to post up their shortest player and I had an easy basket over him for our first score of the game. This was a play coach designed to steal a basket here and there.

With Steeby's injury cutting down his play, we needed something to exploit the mismatch between their short guard and me. But the Inman coach promptly called time out and brought in Kent Neufield, a 6'3" defensive player to replace their shortest player, and I never scored again. Later, that Neufield went to college with a cousin of mine and talked about that State Championship game. It seemed that their coach was very aware of my unique ability, and he had practiced for that possibility. Neufield's coming into the game was no accident! Evidently that Inman coach had his team very well prepared for that game. It wasn't his first "big game" in coaching!

Left to right—Moochie (20), Mike Herndon (32), Steve
Steeby (10), Doug Duncan (40), and Gary Duncan (22)

## Chapter 2

# Mike and Moochie, Baseball and Jobs

Now Mike Teter couldn't play high school sports, but that didn't stop him from being involved in sports. His Dad was a great baseball player! In fact, he's in the Kansas Hall of Fame as one of the best players Kansas ever had! Mike and Moochie (me) both loved baseball! Moochie believed that Mike would have been a great baseball player just like his Dad if he could have had two healthy legs.

After the youth baseball season was over, Mike and Moochie would start another phase of their "baseball love" called the National Baseball Congress Tournament where teams from all over would find their way to Wichita, Kansas. Mike and Moochie also called the baseball stadium, Lawrence Stadium, their own personal "Mecca" of baseball.

August in Wichita meant baseball at the NBC Tournament to Mike and Moochie! To Mike and Moochie (me), it also meant a trip to see not only the former major leaguers but the up and coming stars of tomorrow. Before Mike and Moochie (me) had their own cars, it meant finding a ride to our "Mecca" of baseball! The tickets to those games were easy to get as each night had a business that sponsored the games played that night. Mike and Moochie (me) kept track of that very important item and would school the drivers of possible "rides" as to what those businesses were and where they were located. Having those tickets in hand with extras was imperative in, pardon the pun, "mooching" a ride!

Rock and roll and baseball weren't the only loves of Mike. Mike loved golf as did Moochie (me) but not nearly to the level of Mike's love for it! Mike's love for golf impressed the golf pro at Rolling Hills, Gene O'Brien, so much that he helped Mike become a caddy at Rolling Hills at twelve years old! Mr. O'Brien made things available to Mike for free in order for Mike to be equal to the other caddies in doing the job! Mike joined buddies like Jerry Tiemeyer and others to be the caddies at Rolling Hills Country Club. Mike was in the sixth grade! It was Mike's first paying job!

After the caddy job the next job Mike landed was at the Green Top Café (in the giant green fiberglass roof gas station that Marlene's Dad, Gene Miles, built on West 54). Marlene was another classmate of Mike and Moochie. 54 Highway is now known as Kellogg. The Green Top Café was where Mike washed dishes for thirty-five cents an hour. Mike was fifteen, and for young teens, beggars can't be choosers, but wages like that had to be set during a different time . . . like the dark ages! I don't know how long Mike worked at the Green Top, but at thirty-five cents an hour, one hour would be too much!

Mike's next job couldn't have come quick enough for Mike. By his sophomore year, Mike had learned a little bit about when to be truthful and when to be a little less truthful about his age and he landed a second-shift job at Burnham Fiberglass. Tom Kerns also worked at Burnham, so Goddard High was well represented at Burnham's. Tom was also underage but not as far underage as Mike. In his junior and senior years, Mike landed a job at Precision Winding. Another classmate, Jim Hake, (also known as Mike and Moochie's rock and roll buddy), joined Mike there in their senior year. Then it was off to college for Mike!

In Mike's freshman year at Hutch Juco, he worked at Pepe's Taco for $1.25 an hour. Mike was moving up the corporate ladder, maybe not monetary wise, but by "bennies" (mr). As a side benefit to the job, Mike had free Mexican food and loved every bit of it! Knowing Mike as I did, another "benny" had to be control of what station they listened to while at work. Does anyone doubt what played on that station? College does strange things to kids. Put up a sign with free "Mexican food" for employees on it, in a college town, and then just watch the job become a sought after, desired by all, position (mr)!

"In a little café . . . Just the other side of the border . . . She was just sitting there givin' me looks…That made my mouth water . . . So I started walking her way" . . . Just the thought of Mexican food brings "Jay and The Americans" huge hit *Come a Little Bit Closer* blasting through Moochie's head. Now I have to get a Roy Orbison song to chase it out!

Since we're talking about a beautiful woman, how about Roy Orbison's *Pretty Woman* to chase it out! "Pretty woman walkin' down the street . . . Pretty woman the kind I like to meet . . . Pretty woman I don't believe you, you're not the truth . . . No one could look as good as you . . ." I think that'll do it! Now how do I get that and the thoughts of that beautiful woman out of Moochie's head? Oh well, let it play just a little while longer. Oops, something else is starting to play . . ." The fella rolled down his window . . . And yelled for me to hear . . . Hey buddy how do I get this car outta second gear!" Oh no, not the "Playmates" *Little Nash Rambler* song. What triggered that? MOOCHIE!

# Chapter 3

## Mike, Moochie, and Dennis
## Check Out Denver

In the summer of 1969, Mike was working at Cessna in Hutchinson when they had a two-week vacation. Mike hadn't worked there long enough to get vacation pay. Mike then had a brainstorm, how about taking a "road trip" and check out Denver? Mike knew his college roommate and fellow Goddard graduate, Dennis, didn't have a job. He knew Moochie (me) had just taken his physical for the service and had flunked it. He also knew Moochie had just left Denver to take that physical. So the brainstorm was taking shape.

Moochie (me) still had a job in Denver roofing houses. Dennis had worked in roofing with Moochie (me). Piece of cake, let's go! So Dennis joined Mike and Moochie (me) on the trip to Denver that took two days and all of the trio's money except small change. Dennis, Mike, and Moochie (me) found out about depression on that "road trip," not the mental kind but The Depression! Like how living in The Depression of the thirties had to have been like!

What should've been a "piece of cake" turned into a nightmare! First we blew out a tire. We didn't have a "usable" spare, so we had to buy a tire. There went money we intended for other things. Mike's 1960 Ford was not only a used car but a very "used-up car!" There were so many things that were threatening to go out that we should have put a sign on it that said "please steal," and we would be way ahead after it was stolen! Three bus tickets to Denver and back would have been cheaper! We also learned why Fords were called by the phrase "Ford: Fix or Repair Daily." Okay, probably not new Fords but used ones or in this case "used-up ones!"

So, we were out the money for a tire already! The car's water pump was getting close to being known as "junk!" When we left Wichita, it was leaking water, and we could only go about thirty miles before it would need water. By the time we hit I-70, the miles between stops had dropped and by Hays, Kansas, it was down to being an "every exit stop for water!" We were halfway, and the second half looked like the moon away.

Mike was the only one of the group that wanted to continue, and unfortunately, when Mike makes up his mind, he was "stubborn" to get to where he was going or "die" trying! I think it was that "die trying" that bothered Dennis and Moochie (me) the most. We decided to get a few beers in Hays and consider our options. We were ripe, not for a new idea, we were RIPE! We hadn't run the AC because of the failing water pump; we stunk!

As we sat drinking beers, you could tell Dennis was getting relaxed and back into his element, girls and a college town. Dennis had gone all day without seeing, talking, or anything else with girls! He had definitely not been in his comfort zone; now he was! He was in a college town, and his mind was no longer on that hot and dusty I-70 headed to Denver!

I had known Dennis even longer than I knew Mike, but I could not see what made him attractive to all the girls. Oh well, go get 'em, Dennis, and get Mike and Moochie (me) a place to crash for the night! Which Dennis did! The term "crash" was "hippie speak" for a place to sleep, either because of the body needing it or because of stressful situations and our trio fit both! It could be a bed, a cot, or just a place on the floor! I did not know if Dennis scored with either girl, but frankly I didn't care. Neither Mike nor Moochie (me) was keeping score!

The next day, we bought a water pump and got it installed! Denver seemed a lot closer than it had been the night before. We believed that if nothing else happened, we had enough gas money to reach Denver, and we did! We actually arrived in Denver with some money left over! We put a couple of dollars of gas in the tank and still had enough left over for supper and a room at the Rolling Stone Motel! They were cottages, not exactly what we Kansas "hicks" called a motel.

But whatever, it was a room with beds and what we really needed, a shower! I called my boss to see if I still had a job, and if I did, was there a house ready for me and my new "partner" to roof? I did still have my job, and he gave me directions to a house that was ready to roof. So far so good! We may have been out of "folding money," but we had made it to Denver, and we had a job! Dennis took his shower and laid down on one of the beds, and by the time Mike and Moochie (me) finished our showers, Dennis was snoring away!

Things were right again in the world! We had been concentrating so much on just getting to Denver that we went a little crazy spending what little money we had but we had made it! (mr) Mike and Moochie (me) went over to a gas station around the corner from the motel. We had bought some gas there when we first arrived in Denver, and the young man there had been pleasant, so we kept him company during his shift. He was Mexican, but we had no problem with that; both Mike and Moochie loved Mexican food, so we did have something in common to talk about. So we talked and talked, becoming if not, best friends, and then pretty good ones! He asked where we were from, so we talked about Kansas and our trip to Denver.

The next morning, using my boss's directions, we found the house. It was a new house that had just been framed so Dennis and Moochie (me) started roofing it. Mike took the car and went out to do a search for his job. We roofers had enough change to get a loaf of bread and bologna for lunch. When Mike got back, he had a ten-dollar bill and a story for us roofers.

Mike had gone on an interview with a head of personnel at a plant. The guy's name brought instant recognition to Mike, and to Moochie later on, Lionel Taylor of Denver

Broncos fame. He had caught over a hundred passes in one season! Mike said he did well on a machinist test he completed for Mr. Taylor. But the boss of the section Mike would work in "didn't want a cripple."

This disappointed Mr. Taylor, but Mike had told him of our predicament, and he gave Mike a ten-dollar bill. That night we had pork and beans, Vienna sausage, and saltines. It was a meal fit for a king! Mike slept in the car that night; Dennis and Moochie (me) slept in the house we were roofing. So far, this "piece of cake" trip reminded me of the stories my Dad told of how he and his brother Bill survived during The Depression!

The next day we continued roofing, and Mike once again went looking for a job. Dennis and Moochie (me) were not roofing very fast as maybe our diet and conditions were taking their toll on us. Mike got back, and we had a late lunch. The progress on the roof was slow, but we knew we could finish the next day. We did finish the next day and started to my boss's house in north Denver. The house we had finished roofing was south of Denver, and our gas gauge was near zero! On our first day in Denver, we had stopped at this gas station, and later that day we came back and spent time striking up a friendly relationship with the attendant.

So we went back to that station hoping we had at least made a good impression with that attendant. We had a small favor we hoped he could help us on . . . Would he loan us five dollars in gas to get to my boss's house? We even offered to put up our spare tire for collateral. The hours we had spent talking to him were not wasted; we learned a lot about him, and he did the same about us! He said he would; he trusted us and gave us the gas without the collateral. That was a good thing because the spare tire we had was the one that blew out getting to Denver. If he had seen that tire, he might have backed out thinking we were trying to cheat him. But his actions would all prove to benefit him later that night.

With the gas in our tank, we headed up to north Denver to collect the $84 for the job. After cashing the check, we immediately went back to "our" new buddy at the station to give him the five dollars he had loaned us in gas! We then pulled out on Federal Blvd and looked for a place to eat. We were starving! The first place Mike saw was a Mexican restaurant. Did I tell you Mike loved Mexican food?

This was not a Taco Tico or even a Tex-Mex restaurant; this was a real Mexican restaurant! Even the menu was in Spanish! Now I had taken three years of Spanish, but the last year I took it only to ogle Miss Schultz! She was our young and beautiful Spanish teacher, and she was just a few years older than us. I was more like the character on *Hogan Heroes* Sgt. Schultz who was always saying, "I know nothing, I know nothing," than anything that beautiful woman tried to teach me about speaking Spanish. Mike ordered first, and after he did, I said, "That sounds good to me." Huevos rancheros turned out to be a fried egg on top of chili. We were hungry, so we ate it all!

We then went to see Lionel Taylor to pay him back the ten dollars. We really needed showers, so we went back to the cottage rental motel by our "new buddy's gas station."

The Rolling Stone Motel had what we desperately needed once again, a shower! Once again Dennis took his shower and went to bed and slept! Mike and Moochie (me) went over to the gas station to visit with "our now proven friend."

A car pulled into the station and wanted a quart of oil put into the engine. There were six guys in the car. Our Mexican buddy did exactly that and told the driver, "That will be eighty-five cents, please." The driver screamed, "Eighty-five cents!" and climbed out of the car to confront the station's attendant, our new buddy!

The Mexican attendant, our friend, wisely backed all the way up to the front of the station and us. In this situation you don't want to be where you are surrounded. The driver, the leader of what we figured out now was a gang, slammed the attendant, our friend, back into the glass of the front of the station. I had seen the others climb out of the car with chains and tire tools in hand. Our new buddy was not going to like what they were going to do to him.

But he was our buddy, so I loudly said, "Back off," and the driver (leader) turned his attention to me, uh oh, now I was going to be his target! But the attendant had helped us in our time of need, so I was not going to stand by and watch this gang beat up or do worse to my friend! So I stepped forward to square off with the leader; sometimes we just don't think before opening up our mouths! But he was my friend and had proven that! My friend, after I stepped up, went back inside the station. I didn't have time to think about that or judge his actions. I had my own battle now! My thoughts were pretty simple . . . don't go down! At least as long as I don't go down or not knock him down either, it might stay just one-on-one. At least that was my hope.

Then I looked over at my other buddy, Mike; he had a pop bottle in his hand. If one of the gang would get close enough, I knew Mike was going to clobber him. I wanted to yell at him to stop, but yelling at Mike would only bring attention to him and his intentions. While my attention was on Mike, my opponent landed a pretty good one on me. I didn't go down, but it staggered me. Just then we heard the sirens; the police were on their way!

The gang members ran to their car and peeled out of the station. A few seconds after that the police with red lights and sirens screaming went right on by! And those police cars were going the wrong way! They were not coming to stop the hoods from beating us senseless. They were answering another call! Just after the siren faded away, the station was overrun by Mexicans, our new buddy had made a phone call, and his buddies were responding! There was a tense moment when they saw two white guys. Those two white guys were us, Mike and Moochie, and our buddy, our friend, started screaming something in Spanish. After that, everything was good!

## Chapter 4

# Mike and Moochie, Pat and Kay

Dennis left the next day and hitchhiked back to Wichita; I think the whole adventure was not like he thought it would be, and to be honest I didn't blame him one bit! (mr) The piece of cake road trip turned into a version of *The Grapes of Wrath*, and unfortunately "Henry Fonda" was not going to step out of the movie and make things better for us. Dennis became discouraged, and I doubt he called it an exciting adventure!

For Mike and Moochie (me), it probably fit us better, as we seemed to like living on the edge and taking risks, we liked challenges and adventure of that life! Mike and Moochie bounced around Denver with various addresses. Mike found a good job, and Moochie (me) would turn in his roofing hatchet for a framing hammer and start a journey in the carpentry field. After some split-ups, Mike and Moochie (me) found themselves at 13th and Vine. Wilbur Harrison would have been proud . . . "I'm gonna be standing on the corner Twelfth Street and Vine . . . With

my Kansas City baby and bottle of Kansas City wine" . . .
"Kansas City" . . . Wilbur Harrison!

In the late 1960s and early 1970s, it may be a shock, but both Moochie (me) and Mike smoked "pot" but during that time in Denver, and just about all the young people did! For young people at that time in Denver, not smoking pot would have had a very restricting effect on their having other young friends. I did not smoke as much as most of the young people, but I was a frequent pot smoker. Mike and Moochie (me) lived in an old house that had been converted into apartments. The area was perfect for the young people who flocked to Denver at that time. The rent was cheap, and there was a large park nearby that attracted a lot of "hippie chicks!" For some reason young boys want young girls around! So it was perfect for young people like Mike and Moochie (me)!

We may have lived on the third floor, but we spent as much time in the other apartments as we did in ours. On the second floor lived Pat and Kay, a couple of girls from Grand Island, Nebraska, who were about a year younger or so but pretty much our age. In fact just about everyone in Denver at that time was about our age! With Pat and Kay, we became good friends. Mike and Moochie (me) both held jobs and went to work every day. Pat and Kay lived the "hippie lifestyle" and did not work.

Kay had a brother who was a dope dealer. Pat and Kay got their money from him by being the "middleman" or in this case "woman" for small dope deals with their friends, which sometimes was us. I think the girls saw it as performing a community service. Their friends wanted dope, mostly pot, and the girls knew a dope dealer (Kay's brother)! Everything was "great!" The girls were great company, and they became our dates to concerts and other adventures in the Denver area. It was at those concerts where the girls carried our wine in their very large purses! The concerts were often at "Red Rocks," a natural amphitheater in the foothills west of Denver, and the entrance was uphill all the way! Yes, those two girls were worth the price of admission anywhere we went!

We even went to "drive-in" movies on "half price night." Half price night was any night as Mike and Kay would sit in the front seat of Mike's El Camino. In the back, Pat and I would be under the snap on tarp with our folding chairs! One time after Mike snapped us in, Pat said it was lucky she was not pregnant as Mike would have never got it snapped in that case, never being one who passes on an opportunity I answered, "You're not out of here yet, Pat!" Lucky we were not near the entrance as they would have definitely heard the laughter then!

Many times Kay would slide the small window open and tell us to be quiet in a very stern voice as we neared the entrance to the drive-in. We would answer her warning with a "yes, mother!" We then tried to stifle the laughter with our hands over our mouths. I guess sometimes we would laugh so much that Kay was sure that we would blow our cover! Not only did we never get thrown out, but we began to believe the people taking the admission money didn't care or maybe they were just entertained by our antics. That possibility might have been backed up by Mike unsnapping the tarp and the calmness of Pat and me as we set up our folding chairs in the back bed of Mike's El Camino to watch the movie. We did not hide our actions, and nobody in the drive-in even said anything.

Other days or nights, the four of us, like all young people, really liked pizza, and we would go out to "our pizza" place, "Straight Johnsons," at least once a week. Sometimes, we also went up to "Sam's Place," a 3.2 bar on "Lookout Mountain," to take in and dance to local groups like "Love Special Delivery" (LSD) and some other local rock and roll groups. Groups and businesses at that time used names that were drug related, like "Straight Johnson's and Love Special Delivery." Life was good and really fun in Denver during those times for full-time hippies and part-time, like Mike and Moochie, as we had jobs and did not have the appearance of hippies. (mr) But the good things changed one day.

One day when I got home from work, I was very tired. So tired I barely managed the climb up the first stairway. As I reached the second floor, I was given a reprieve. The door to the girls' apartment was open. It usually was open if the girls were home. So I could take a rest before going up to our apartment on the third floor. Mike was there already in the girls' apartment (he had gone to the liquor store on Colfax and bought a bottle of Bali Hai), so I walked in, poured myself a glass, and sat down on the girls' couch.

The pay phone in the hall rang, and Mike went to answer it. It was the girl he was trying to get to go with him to a concert in Greeley. Somewhere during this time, I lay down and dozed off on the girls' couch. A commotion woke me up to discover a gun barrel pointing at my face!

Not a good way to wake up! Mike was still on the phone giving the girl on the other end of the line play-by-play of what he was witnessing directly in front of him. Mike later told me of what he had watched, as three ratty looking guys and one ratty looking chick came into view at the top of the first stairway. They were pretty much the normal-looking visitors to our apartment building, maybe a little older, but old hippies are people too!

They had walked up the hall toward Mike and suddenly turned into the girls' open door. They turned out to be four of "Denver's finest" vice detectives! We got a close and very personal view that day of the war on drugs in Denver in the early 1970s! Most young people, especially in Denver, did not consider smoking pot a real crime. I think many of the DPD looked upon busting hippies as an easy bust, low-hanging fruit, easy scalps, and easy road to advancement. At what cost to the kids who didn't even consider it a crime, who cares they're kids, and worse than that, they're hippies!

We never found out who set the girls up and got me arrested. It was most likely a poor hippie who was busted and was most likely promised a lesser charge if he or she "ratted out" who and where he or she bought the dope. This would certainly fit the girls' involvement and most likely the scene of the "buy." The Denver Police must have had a list of the people to arrest as they asked Mike for identification, and after checking it, they walked right past Mike. I didn't think about that then, but they never asked me for ID. The way they acted toward me with gun drawn and in my face, they must have already known who and what I was.

They walked down the hall pulling another young person out of his apartment. It was at the end of the hall, with the door closed. They arrested him, too! Mike who was right outside the girls' apartment on the hall phone was not arrested. I guess the joker in the deck was me! It was obvious later on that I wasn't the guy who they thought I was! I think what they must have thought was that they had the brother, the dope dealer! They had instead the guy who held a job and pounded nails for his living not the dope dealer. AND I probably cared more for those two girls than he did! I think that was proven later.

So then it became handcuff time for the four arrested. We were split up with one girl and me in one police car and the same in the other police car. On the ride to the police station, the "officers" showed their true nature. They went on and on about how much "free love" sex we must have had with each other. Then one added that he had heard that most hippies didn't care which gender they had sex with, opposite or same sex. He added that it made him sick. I'll never forget that ride to the police station! Both of us were terrified, and these two were enjoying each moment of our terror! It was a real eye-opener to see the type of people who chose "to serve and protect" at that time!

After that, things got a little weird for me. After a day in the Denver city jail, I was transferred to the county jail. I didn't see anyone for a week! I wasn't brought up before a judge. I wasn't charged for anything; no bail was set. Mike went to the jails, and they swore they didn't have me! I didn't exist according to them! According to the jailhouse lawyers, fellow inmates, I couldn't be there if everything I said was true! They didn't believe me.

I guess my boss came looking for me after a few days, and he could not find me either in the jails. I guess I was a problem that they could not solve. After it became obvious I wasn't the prize as they first thought, but then who was this person? I think after a few days, I just became lost in the system. The house that my boss and his crew (including me) were working on was a lawyer's home. That may have been when my luck changed. The lawyer said he would find me. All this time I could only think about the girls that I was arrested with. Finally the lawyer found me! I guess I existed after all!

Oops, I hear a song bouncing around in Moochie's head . . .

"I'm breakin' rocks in the hot sun . . . I fought the law and the law won . . . I miss my baby and I feel so bad . . . I guess my race is run . . . Oh, she's the best girl I've ever had . . . I fought the law and the law won." It was *I Fought the Law* by the Bobby Fuller Four that was bouncing around in Moochie's head!

# Chapter 5

# Mike and Moochie, Lawyers
# and the Rolling Stones

My lawyer told me the girls had been charged for possession with intent to sell. I asked what the girls would be facing if they were found guilty. He said that wasn't what he was hired to do; I was his only concern. He did say that the intent to sell charge probably meant some jail time. He could at least see my concern, but he quickly moved back to my case. On my case he said with the way my arrest and the foul-ups after were handled, I could sue and easily win.

I told him to make a deal instead, and that deal had to include the girls. My attorney was not real happy, but I had that week in jail to think things over in my head; I wasn't afraid anymore. I let my concern for the girls be foremost in my mind; nothing else mattered, and it had become one of those . . . in a hundred years . . . things for me . . . third person-type stuff. I could be focused and very stubborn in third person mode!

My lawyer fought me, but by now, he probably just wanted to get it done and out of his hair and off of his hands! I told him I would even plead no contest to a charge that would result in probation if the girls would get the same. After the prosecutor quickly agreed to the terms, I thought my case against the city must have been pretty good, but the girls only got probation, and they were my main concern!

Many lives were ruined by kids serving time in Colorado jails. I didn't want that to happen to our friends, two really nice girls! Their real crime was their wanting to live the hippie lifestyle so badly that they took a big risk and got involved with a family member's business in order to have that lifestyle. The crime might have been having a real-life creep for a brother.

The girls did have to come back for a court appearance. We had to pick them up at the train station. The train was set to roll into the station around 7:00 a.m. which caused us to do a little rearranging in our usual activities. We had moved out of the 13th and Vine apartments by mutual agreement with the powers that be and us. I don't think they liked us being the reason for bringing the vice cops to their building! They didn't like us getting busted there, and neither did we, so we moved to Evergreen.

To Mike and Moochie, Evergreen was the most beautiful place in the "world." We rented a place on Upper Bear Creek Road for a thousand a month. There were four of us, so the rent was manageable. The place was rented for about four times that during the summer months, and it was beautiful. It might have been the highlight of Mike and Moochie's time in Denver.

Evergreen was a beautiful small mountain town with a couple of great bars, like the "Little Bear Inn," to spend nights dancing! Sam's Place on Lookout Mountain was nearby also, and we took full advantage of it! Red Rocks, in the foothills west of Denver, was just minutes away. The concerts held there were easy to get to from our Evergreen apartment. And the groups we saw there were the name groups of that era! What more could you want? We wished we could afford to live there in Evergreen, year round!

The only drawback to Evergreen was that it was too far away to go home after work and return back to Denver later. At least that was what we told ourselves the reason was! Actually it would cut down on our partying by having to be somewhere at 7:00 a.m. which would have been impossible for us to do by partying in Evergreen! If we had to pick up the girls at the train station early in the morning, we would have to party in Denver! So that is what we did!

We did get to the train station a little before the train with the girls on board, LIKE about five hours! We spent the time, as we waited for the train, sleeping on hard wooden benches in the station until the train arrived. If you're drunk enough, you can sleep anywhere!

It just so happened that the Nebraska Cornhuskers were playing a football game against the Colorado Buffalos that weekend in Boulder. When the train rolled into the station, the drunks, all wearing red jackets and strawhats, also rolled in with the train and off, as many of them actually did roll off and laid there until a fellow "Cornhusker" helped them stand! There were hundreds of them! It was a sight to behold, as almost every one of them was very drunk! It could have been called "falling down drunk" for many of the "Cornhusker Nation" that day!

Although both the girls and Moochie (me) got probation, the girls' parents got their probation moved to their hometown in Nebraska. It was probably needed by the girls; they probably didn't think so at the time. But it moved them away from a very dangerous place for them! As the DPD would have had the girls "marked as targets" as long as they were in Denver. I had learned a lot about the habits of the "cops" during my stay in the county Hilton!

I didn't think I would ever see them again. But we kept communicating through letters, and finally I got a letter from Pat asking me to buy some tickets to The Rolling Stones/Stevie Wonder America Tour when it came through Denver! After getting the tickets, I wrote and told them that they had to come then as the tickets were $12 a piece! I would have paid that many times over just to see them again! They wrote back and asked if I could pick them up at the train station on the morning of June 16!

I had bought four tickets; my head wasn't working real well as Mike had gotten married to Betty Jo . . . After thinking a little bit, I decided I had an extra ticket as I didn't think Betty Jo would appreciate me setting up a date with another woman for her husband. Moochie had really messed up. When I bought the tickets, it was always the four of us in my mind: Pat and Kay, Mike and Moochie! But now it wasn't, it was Pat, Kay, and me (Moochie)!

Now another thing came in to play. I had forgotten about another friend from Goddard who was coming to Denver around that time. In fact, he called me a couple of nights before the concert after getting into Denver. His name was Richard, and he was calling me from the "Cat and Fiddle," a bar on Broadway. The "Cat and Fiddle" was not a place I would recommend to anyone that didn't know the "lay of the land so to speak!" Richard said that he just stopped at the first bar he saw to "have a cold one" and call to get directions to my apartment. It seems Richard had another problem besides directions, a "giant black man!" I guess Richard was like normal guys from Goddard; they didn't have any sense in urban settings! Richard said, before he called me, that he had gone up to the bar and ordered a "cold one." As he took out his wallet to pay, he noticed a "huge black man" looking inside his wallet! Now Richard, like many "hicks from Kansas," had every bit of the money he brought for his time in Denver in full display to the "giant!"

Now the parking for the bar was in the back, "in the dark." Richard was sure he would never live past that parking lot! I told him to wait in the bar; I'd come down, and maybe with two of us we could watch each other's back and "escape!" So I went the couple blocks over to the bar. I found Richard sitting in a booth. As I walked over, I noticed the "big black giant" looking at me.

I sat down with Richard and said, "Welcome to Denver, man." Before I could start on my "dos and don'ts" of how to act in this type of urban setting, Richard, whose eyes had never left the "giant black man," said, "He's coming over." The "big black giant" sat down beside Richard across from me. Richard had scooted over to the wall and could go no further! The "giant" looked at me and said, "Steve, what's happening?" I responded, "Not too much, Spence, how are you doing?" Then Spence looked over at Richard, and I introduced them to each other.

To be truthful, I had known who the "big black giant" was before I entered the bar. But the game had to be played out! Spence told Richard of the mistakes Richard made in buying his beer and what Spence called "flashing his billfold" where everybody could see! I knew when I walked in I was in no real danger as the other "big black giant" that stopped at that bar was Spence's boss, Ron Lyle. Big Ron was the fourth ranked heavyweight in the "world" at that time! Ron Lyle would fight the world's champion, George Foreman, in an epic fight that featured five knockdowns! Two of those were Ron Lyle knockdowns of George Foreman! Unfortunately, the other three were by George Foreman including the knockout! Spence's connection with Ron Lyle was that he was Ron Lyle's sparring partner. Ron Lyle and Spence were about the same size. AND yes they were "big black giants!" To me, they were nice guys.

Now I had known Spence for a while, not in any boxing sense, but Spence's lady, who he lived with, was my partner's future mother-in-law. And I have to admit that Spence did scare me with our first meeting! Spence and my partner's future mother-in-law could have had a common-law marriage as the relationship had lasted for years. But she had said they couldn't afford to get married. I couldn't buy that reason; it may have been just cold feet on one of their parts, but it didn't involve me! Mixed couples had never bothered me; I was from Kansas. Kansas was basically where the Civil War against slavery started, Bloody Kansas, the 1850s, duh.

Spence wasn't my only black friend. When I lived at the 13th and Vine apartment, I would go the one block to the Aladdin bar. It was mostly a black bar, meaning that those who frequented it were mostly black. I spent enough time in there that I was accepted by the other patrons of it. In fact I was the "shortstop" on the bar's team that played fast pitch softball, in a league there in Denver. I was also a halfback on the bar's flag football team. And I was the "point guard" on our basketball team!

At parties that centered around the bar's teams, I was usually the only white guy there. Ducie Henry, our first baseman, a lineman (THE line) of our football team, and the center on our basketball team, warned me that somebody may not know me and basically pick me to beat up. Ducie told me to just holler and he (6'8" 280) would handle the problem. Of course there were other Henrys around like James who played third base, quarterback, and big forward. James was only 6'6" and 230. There was another Henry that played catcher, tight end and shooting guard. So, although Ducie had warned me, I never had any problems . . . of course when you walk in with the Henrys, that alone might have made a pretty loud statement!

Now, I think my teammates considered me "their" shortstop, "their" point guard, "their" halfback without the color distinction! I was of the same mind toward them. I recognized them for their contribution to "our" team, no color, just teammates! One for all, all for one; if a fight would have started, I knew they would have my back and

I would have theirs! I, along with the three Henrys, were voted onto the Fast Pitch All-Star Team. My youngest brother, Bob, came out for a visit, so I took him with me to one of our flag football games. Brother Bob got to witness Ducie, as he kicked a 68-yard field goal in that flag football game. Bob also got to witness an all ABA guard, Ralph Simpson, make a complete fool out of me in one of our basketball games. I often wondered how the white guard felt who played for the team that played against the Globetrotters; that day I found out! Oh well, the team and I had fun! The opposing team was not the Globetrotters, but they were close. That team was made up of ABA's (professional team members) Denver Rockets! How did we end up playing in that league? Well, we had gone undefeated in our "rec" league, and the Denver Rockets needed a team to fill out their summer league. After that one game both us and them decided we were not at a level to give them a useful practice let alone a game.

So with Richard in Denver, I had a "user" for the spare ticket. I got to renew our friendship, between the girls and me, by way of the mail: Stevie Wonder and the Rolling Stones! AND, I also had two dates to take to the concert, although Richard got to sit with Kay. I'll always cherish the time I got to be with them! Now there was a foul-up in the announcing of Stevie Wonder and his band that day as his band was called "The Wonderkings." I think that confused Pat as to who the band really was, opening the door for one of my jokes to be played! I think Pat must have thought that it was an opening band to the headlining groups, Stevie Wonder and Rolling Stones. When Pat said, after watching members of Stevie Wonder's band leading Stevie from one instrument to play another instrument, "I think he's blind," I answered, "I believe you're right Pat, in fact, I believe STEVIE WONDER has been blind since birth!" My ability of never letting an opportunity for seeing a joke and acting upon it had returned! Pat did punch my shoulder for trying the joke at her expense, but then she cracked up laughing. She was still Pat, and I was still Moochie! The banter never stopped with Pat and me (Moochie), jokesters to the end. It seemed like we were together, once more, under that tarp in the back of Mike's El Camino, with Kay getting mad at us for our loud laughter!

Those two girls were two of my best friends in Denver; I not only missed them, but I also missed all the good times we had in Denver together! They left early the next morning; they hadn't told anyone of their coming back to Denver. Not their parents, not their probation officer; in fact, just being with me would have broken the terms of their probation, if they were caught with me! They left just as they came. They hadn't changed; they were still risk takers! Of course, just my being with them would have also broken the terms of my probation, that is, if I was caught with them! So I guess none of us had changed, risk takers all!

# Phil, the Fonz, and His Scribe, Moochie

# *Chapter 1*

As we grew older, our games took on a more serious nature. Phil Wohlford moved into Goddard right next door to our house on Spruce Street. I don't know the reason he moved in with his brother there in Goddard; I kind of thought Phil had become too unruly for his Mom and Dad, so maybe that was the reason. Phil was a lot like us, the Knowles boys, so we thought whatever the reason, it was alright with us. But we did have rules of our own, so Phil would now have to obey them, or else! We never ever had anyone who wanted to challenge them, so the "or else" really didn't have any penalty! The first rule: after someone moves into "our" block, the rule on Spruce Street was that we got to inspect the new kid's stuff. My eyes lit up when out from the box came two sets of boxing gloves. Playing "make-believe" was a thing little kids played. We had no use for the "make-believe" stuff, as we had in those boxing gloves, big guy tools.

Now I really don't know what training Phil had in boxing, but it was certainly more than the Spruce Street Gang! Now I, or Moochie as I had carried that nickname since I was seven or eight, was either thirteen or fourteen when Phil moved in next door to our house on Spruce Street. I was the oldest of the gang of Spruce Street kids, as my older brother, Chuck, had been swallowed up by the adult world of work and girls! It was my responsibility to test the new "kid," or guy in this case, on the block.

There actually wasn't a real gang of Spruce Street kids, and we didn't have a set of rules written down anywhere. And if there was, Phil, since he was a couple years older, would have been the leader because of age. But Phil would have been disqualified as Chuck had been, as he was Chuck's age, and if you were focused on anything except the Spruce Street Gang, you couldn't be the leader. Boy these non-rules can get complicated!

If you grew up in the "Knowles" household, in the 1950s, you did have experience concerning boxing. We might have had the first television set on Spruce Street. We quickly found out that the TV in our living room was not there for us kids; it was there so Dad could watch *Friday Night Boxing*! It only took a few knuckle raps to the head of any of us kids to find out standing between Dad and that TV set on Friday night was not smart or healthy. But, we did learn the "lay of the land" concerning that TV! The first knuckle rap would cause pain, but eventually it would pass. The second conviction might cause . . . death or worse! But on the plus side, we also got the *Game of the Week* with Diz an' Pee Wee along with the *World Series*, or as Mom would say, the "World Serious!" So it wasn't all bad!

We, of the "Knowles boys" of the "Spruce Street Gang," did have a lot of experience in the art of boxing, or so we thought. We did have a lot of experience in "watching" boxing! In the Knowles household, as was previously noted, Friday meant *Friday Night Boxing*! We watched

Sugar Ray, Gene and Don Fulmer, Floyd Patterson, Sonny Liston, and, the "new kid" in boxing, Cassius Clay. We also learned the importance of razor blades and headache powder, as between rounds the songs of the commercials would sing out "how are you fixed for blades" and "plop, plop, fizz, fizz, oh, what a relief it is!" (mr) Those ditties would rattle through my head and still do! Gillette and Alka Seltzer with "Speedy" became household words in our vocabulary and in the nation's also! Don Dunphy also became the voice of boxing! "Tonight, we have ten rounds of boxing . . ." We didn't know that there was anything less than ten rounds in boxing!

Oops, I got sidetracked, where were we? Oh yeah, Phil and boxing! As I said, I don't know how much training Phil had received, if he had any. But it was spread around that he had competed in Golden Gloves. If that was a false rumor, it might have been me that created it, not only the initial story but also the spreading of that rumor. I had to save face you see! Now I didn't challenge Phil; you don't challenge anybody that has his own set of boxing gloves! I may be stupid, but not that stupid! I did it a different way; I asked Phil to teach me how to box.

Now we didn't want any parents to see, so we snuck around to the side of the house. You have to realize, I loved watching Sugar Ray and Cassius Clay. I copied the way they bobbed and weaved and danced in the ring. So I'm standing in front of Phil or "dancing" in front of Phil. Phil starts off by saying, "You're open. You're open. You're open." BAM! Then I'm on the ground, and he is asking if I'm okay. Shaking a few cobwebs loose, I said, "I'm okay." I stood up and started to dance again . . . Then I hear "You're open. You're open. You're open." BAM!

At this point, I think Phil might have been getting worried about hurting me, as he really wasn't teaching me how to box but how to take a punch! But I think I got straight As in whatever Phil was teaching! After convincing Phil I was okay, I cautiously started my dance again. I hear "You're open. You're open . . ." but this time . . . before I heard the third . . . You're open, I threw myself backward to avoid the expected punch. Phil hit hard . . . And I couldn't even see where those punches were coming from! They say, "Discretion is the better part of valor" . . . well that may be true, but throwing yourself out of range might be, if not brave, at least smart! Or at least less painful . . . Did I tell you Phil hit hard? Cobwebs . . . Cobwebs . . . Anybody see where that last one came from? Moochie are you here? I need someone to stand in for me! That event of Phil, sort of, teaching me how to box might have caused "Moochie" to actually exist on his own! Look up: *The Dark Half* by Dean Koontz! It is a story of split personality that the "dark half" becomes a person also but with psychotic results.

Phil did hit hard, not only with boxing gloves but on the football field . . . in practice. Every player took note of where "Wolhford" was! Does anybody know what the phrase "clean your clock" meant on the football field? If you were not aware of where "Wolhford" was, you were probably going to find out. Like Moochie (me) did during the boxing escapade in Phil's side yard . . . cobwebs . . . probably brain damage or at least scrambled! Looking back, I probably should have sent the doctor, who wouldn't let me play football, a thank you note! That decision probably kept me from getting the rest of my brains, if I had any, scrambled all over the practice field in Goddard! Thanks Doc!

I said, concerning Phil's football playing days at Goddard, "in practice." It was not because Phil didn't play well in games. They wouldn't let Phil play in the games against other teams! It was supposed to be because Phil transferred in from Cheney, but most of us really thought it was because he was too dangerous to be let out on a football field! At night . . . in the dark . . . Did I tell you Phil hit hard? Oh yeah, I did! "How many fingers am I holding up, Moochie?" Cobwebs, cobwebs . . . Now Phil did practice; in fact, he never missed a practice. But he never got to play in a game! Bad news for our players . . . great news for the opposing players! I had heard that the opposing teams had a lot of "clocks that needed cleaning!" But Phil's cleaning service was closed down for the season.

Now after Phil "cleaned my clock" in his side yard with his boxing gloves, I never challenged him again! But we became great friends, and we still are! We, Goddard High, considered Phil as the "coolest Goddardtonian"; Phil was our "Fonz" before there was a "Happy Days" or a "Fonz." Mike Teter, Jim Hake, and Moochie (me) tried to be cool by hanging around the disc jockeys at KLEO, but Phil didn't have to try to be cool. HE WAS COOL! Look up "cool" in Webster's Dictionary, you'll find a picture of Phil! I swear, look it up!

Phil went out for track one year and might have run the fastest three hundred yards in history. Once again, Phil was cool! And after that accomplishment spread through the school, his legend grew even bigger! It didn't matter that it was in the quarter mile, which is 440 yards and Phil finished last, it was "cool!" If Phil did it . . . it was definitely "cool!" Now the "Fonz" of "Happy Days" was not only portrayed as "cool," he was supposed to have a rep as a fighter that nobody wanted to fool with! Phil wasn't just thought of being a great fighter; he WAS a "great fighter!"

Phil earned his rep a little differently than most "fighters." Since he wasn't a great big guy, many times he was chosen to be the one who the "tough guys" from other schools picked to beat up. Phil's rep hadn't got out to the Wichita schools, so it was a major surprise to many that their big tough fighter had his "clock cleaned" by an unknown "normal-sized" guy from Goddard High!

Phil's reputation grew and grew! At a party, at Rita Schniepp's house, Rita who was also Goddard Class 1967 with Moochie (me). Just a side note, on both Rita and Moochie (me) and the connection in the history of both! Rita and I were born in the same "Dodge City" hospital three days apart! That is just a little "did you know story" of classmate connection before Goddard High. Here's another "did you know story?" Did you know Dana and Moochie (me) attended first grade together at Eureka Elementary in Wichita (actually I wasn't Moochie yet) but don't remember seeing the other there? We both played in the Big Ditch but Dana played south of 54 Highway, and I played north of it! But I don't think it was any of those reasons, I think it was because Dana was a girl. What good are girls I thought at that time? They can't play baseball very well! What good are they? Where was I? Oh, yes the clash between Wichita West and Goddard High.

Now Rita's was a great place to have a party, as the Schniepp's put in swimming pools for their family business (Ultra Modern Pools). During warm summers, the parties included swimming and bathing suits and a lot of shapely girls in those bathing suits! Does anybody hear the alarms going off? Those girls were also mostly from Goddard High. Goddard High had a lot of very shapely and very beautiful girls, at that time. In fact, Miss Teen Wichita, Cindy Johnson, went to Goddard. She was beautiful and . . . let's say very well put together! Ding, ding, do you hear them now? Cindy was also in the Class of '67 with . . . wait for it . . . me AKA Moochie! Cindy also had some dates with Phil. I think her motives were to make Mike Herndon jealous . . . would a fight between Phil and Mike been a match, Or WHAT! Oh well, let's get back to those beautiful girls who attended Goddard High! Being as it was not confined to the 1967 class, sorry girl classmates, you "weren't the only fish in the sea" at Goddard High, but you were our fish! To those with ears, it must have sounded like at least a three-alarm fire then! Ding, Ding . . . Ding!

Now, when two high schools that really don't like each other come together, things can turn "ugly" over anything . . . at any time! Well guess what, IT DID! A West High student blindsided Phil with a Coke bottle. Now Coke bottles of the 1960s were not the plastic Coke bottles of today; they were made with thick glass so the jostling around in the delivery trucks wouldn't break them.

It would take some real force to break a Coke bottle over someone's head.

Now, when two "unbreakable" objects, the Coke bottle and Phil's head, met, something had to give! In this case, both objects received major damage! The Coke bottle broke as it met the crown of Phil's head! Phil's head and, even more so, Phil's face took the brunt of the rearranging, as the broken bottle proceeded down "just a rippin' and cuttin' down Phil's face!" It almost tore off Phil's nose! Now most people would have stopped and tried to stop the bleeding, but Phil was not most people! Phil was "pissed" and like I said about Phil on the football field . . . very DANGEROUS! In seconds, the West High student was on the ground and being pummeled by a very enraged, out-of-control, bleeding all over . . . "Wohlford . . . Philip Wohlford!" "Bond . . . James Bond! Oh, Moochie, now you're going into Bond movies? What next is rattling around in that head of yours? . . . Cartoons?

After being a spectator for most of the confrontation, my older brother, Chuck, decided this was getting critical. No, not Phil's bleeding, but the consequences of Phil beating the West High student to death. So he and a couple others from Goddard High started pulling Phil away from the "target" of Phil's rage with a statement of truth on many levels . . . "Phil, you're drowning him, we need to take you to the hospital." Yes, Phil was drowning him . . . in Phil's own blood! The Legend of Phil Wohlford grew larger at Rita's party that night!

Now the entire "Legend of Wohlford" is much larger than one story. Just about everyone at Goddard High had a Phil story; in fact if you knew Phil you probably had your own favorite "Phil Wohlford" story! If you really, really knew Phil and hung around with Phil, you probably had many more! Well I lived next door to Phil, knew him, and I still know him as after 50 plus years he is still one of my closest friends. In fact Phil came to Denver on his "honeymoon" with his bride Judy, stopping to visit with Mike Teter, aka "Mike," and I, aka "Moochie!" I don't know what that ritual means in the animal world. It may be a way for the "male of the species" to introduce his "chosen mate" to his friends for their inspection and to also give the "hands off" sign to those friends. Or for the "male" to give a crash course to his "chosen mate" in inspecting his friends. It is that "thumbs up" moment "thing" from whichever was to do the inspecting of whoever! But the key words about this are "his friends!"

I was also a participant in many of the "Wohlford Stories" as they happened.

Now, I was never a "key" member of the "Phil Stories" as the other participants, in listing who were there, would go through the names and always after a pause added "and Moochie" was also there! I guess my job was to be the 'scribe" of the "Phil Legend," kind of like the "on scene reporter of the action!" The "Vin Scully" giving "play by play," the "Walter Cronkite" reporting the news. So, my "Phil Wohlford" collection of stories may be the most complete of anybody's.

When the "key members," who were there, meet and "replay" their "Phil Wohlford Story" for the group to also relive that "adventure," it always starts with "remember when Phil" . . . which always reminds me of a funny story of that period from *Readers Digest*. It was during lunch at a prison, the inmates would, one at a time, stand up and call out a number. After which, all the inmates would laugh with some of them even slapping their knee as if to say "that was a good one!" A new addition to the prison community asked the inmate next to him, after an inmate stood and called out another number that brought no laughs, no knee slapping, no reaction at all, "Why, why the different reaction?" The seasoned inmate replied, "Some people can tell a joke . . . some can't!" The inmates had heard all the jokes before, so the inmates just said the number of the joke that they chose to tell! So if Jerry, or another classmate, does not go into a belly shaking, knee slapping fit after you tell a "remember when" Phil story . . . sit back down and work on your delivery! Or get pointers from Jerry, as he can tell a story like no one else can!

## Chapter 2

# The Further Adventures of Phil and Scribe, Moochie

At this next "Phil" story, I was not actually there; I just have been told it so many times that it also became a favorite without me even being there! The main key participants were, of course Phil . . . my brother, Chuck, and Moochie's 1967 classmate, David. I think, by this time, Moochie and I had become two different people or at least two different personalities. Maybe from a boxing exhibition on Phil's side yard long ago! Did I tell you that Phil hit hard? Oh yeah, I did! Cobwebs . . . But anyway back to the story.

The place was a street called Douglas. The activity was what every high school student from the city of Wichita and its surrounding area did at least once in their life! "Dragging Douglas" was what high school kids called it and did, at least on a Friday or Saturday night! It was like a rite of passage. Guys would form groups, usually with four high school kids in each group. It wasn't a date-type activity as guys were basically out to find either a fight between the occupants of the other car or a race between the drivers. The girls were there to see what happens and hope for boys from other schools to notice them so they could make their boyfriends jealous and appreciate them more. It was like a primal dance!

Since Douglas had stop lights at every block, a race meant leaving Douglas to find a place to hold the race! So actual racing between cars seldom happened! But fights were numerous on a Friday or Saturday night! How to get the four guys in the other car as opponents was very primal also. With stop lights at each block and traffic very thick, it was a stop at every light time thing. In the other lane beside you was another car with guys or girls in it! If there were girls, the guys on that side of the car would put out overtures for the girls to "park around the next corner" and join them swapping two guys for two girls. Sometimes this swapping took place right on Douglas at stop lights. This usually didn't happen unless a girl was in the middle of a fight with her boyfriend! Or wanted to make him "very" jealous or "very" angry as cars would always be lined up across from each other and there was no hiding of who was with whom!

Now the schools were identified by the guys wearing letter jackets. Or by bumper stickers on the cars or on the rear window. Most kids knew where the occupants of the other cars were from, and who held "reps" for fighting were also usually known, USUALLY! If it were guys across from you, the war of insults was on! There is an art to this. When the guy across from you hurls an insult, hurl your own and always stay on the offensive. As long as it stays just being banter between roosters, they and you will tire of the back-and-forth and go to another target at the next light. Now, if two cars holding kids who live for the "thrill of fighting" and they end up across from each other, the fight becomes imminent.

After setting the stage for the play, we now have to tell the story of the main players of the play. Phil was the driver, Chuck was "shotgun," front seat by the window, and David "manned" the back seat and both windows there! Usually, the car held two in the back, but with David there, the group felt even better as David was 6'2" and about 240 lbs. With David in back seat, there wasn't a lot of room or need for that forth person! This is a good use of numbers as from the back it appears the car is short a member and very few times does anybody notice the size of people in the back seat.

Well, a group of East High students pulled alongside and started their line of "not so flattering" remarks. Chuck shot back some answering remarks matching theirs. Phil got their attention with his opinion of East. Phil wasn't a talker, but what was being set up was perfect for his contribution. The East High students would find out what it was! Meanwhile, David just sat quietly in the back seat. This wasn't unusual as the back seat usually held freshman or sophomores, "rookies" to "dragging Douglas" and in fights! Inside the East High car, the driver started making motions with his hand that meant they were ready to settle the difference of opinion and Phil should take the next side street to do the battle! Following some hand motions from Chuck to the car behind the East High car to let Phil's car into its place, that car slowed and Phil drove his car into that space. Phil's car was now behind the

East High car. Phil could now follow that car in making the turn onto the side street. This was standard operating procedure for cars on Douglas . . . let the warring cars fight if they want to! The only difference was that car that had given its place for Phil's car also turned and followed the "warring cars" onto the side road! Not a good sign! I don't think they were just observers!

Chuck said they didn't notice the rear car until after he and Phil had jumped out to do battle with the first car's occupants. Chuck said his fight with his man was about equal. Chuck would land a punch only to have his opponent land one of his own. Phil had already put one out of the battle and was proceeding to do the same to the other. Evidently Phil's reputation hadn't made it to East High . . . yet! I'm sure that changed after this encounter! Chuck was able to avoid his man's punches as they were tiring and both then agreed to a draw. That gave Chuck a chance to check out the car that followed Phil's, and evidently it also held East High kids! But they were just sitting on their car's hood!

David explained later how those East High kids had suddenly lost their desire to fight. David said he had to think of something as he was outnumbered at least four to one. He said it was one of those moments to put on the biggest bluff he could muster. So he turned to face the East High kids from the second car, ripped off his shirt, and addressed the East High student section with an invite to join him in the fight, with a challenge mixed in with some very descriptive adjectives. That group returned to their car and sat on their car's hood. Although David had called it a bluff, I don't think any of those kids wanted to be the first to take on someone of David's size and ATTITUDE! Nobody wanted any part of the enraged giant that he now appeared to be!

Hulk Hogan, the wrestler, had flair, dramatically ripping off his shirt in his WWF matches. When I saw Hulk Hogan rip his shirt off, it reminded me of the flair that David showed with the ripping off his shirt that evening. Since "Hulk Hogan" came on the scene later, maybe he copied David! Maybe some East High student that was there told a story of the "giant" who scared a whole school into submission one summer night in Wichita, Kansas! Thinking back, David did look a lot like the "Shrek" character of cartoon movie fame . . . maybe it wasn't "Hulk Hogan" but some writer/movie-type person, originally from the plains states . . . who either heard the story or actually witnessed it and wrote the "Shrek" story! Can we sue for "origin of idea?" How much should we sue for? Oops, sorry Phil, I got off subject. This is supposed to be about you! But you know how scatterbrained Moochie can get, as you probably caused the scattering of Moochie's brain, in the side yard . . . with the wrench . . . in the dark . . . oh boy, where did that come from? Was it clue? . . . the board game or the movie? There was NO wrench! And it wasn't dark! Let's get back to wherever . . . But David was a "mega friend" to both of us, and I love telling the "David part," so maybe you'll forgive Moochie or whatever the "me" is that caused it! Confused, I know both Moochie and me are very confused! We always ARE! Did I tell you Phil hit hard? Oh . . . yeah . . . I did! I think so?

# Chapter 3

## Phil and His Scribe, Moochie

The next Phil story starts with a term "road hunting" which in most places is illegal. Kansas is one of those places! Another term used for it is the "lazy man's way to hunt!" It is definitely that! Kind of like the opening scene of *Crocodile Dundee II* where Dundee illustrates the "lazy man's way to fish" in the New York harbor . . . with dynamite! With the "Lady in the Harbor" watching every fish die and shedding a tear for each one that did! It's a wonder that Dundee didn't get a "life sentence!" But Crocodile Dundee was a lot like "our" Phil, a very cool and likeable guy, so although the police officers probably did not agree with his "crimes," they probably did laugh at his antics of doing them!

The style of "our road hunting" was not only illegal but had many elements of stupidity! First thing we put our fully loaded shotguns in the car. Then we bought a case of beer as we didn't know if we would see anything to kill. So we needed something to do while driving the dirt roads around Goddard, so we drank beer to pass the time! So with both the shotguns loaded and us "getting loaded," road hunting became a very stupid and very dangerous activity! Then, if you add into this the decisions made while drinking beer, it adds another thing, mob mentality! People egging people on to do something stupid! That always seems to guarantee that something stupid will happen, and it did!

Phil was the driver. Road hunting has some element of just a scenic drive in the country. Phil drove slowly over a small bridge that went over a creek that connected two small ponds. As we reached near the center of the bridge one of our "road hunting" conspirators, Ron yelled, "Stop, I just saw something!" We climbed out of Phil's car going up to the guard rail on the bridges' edge and looked down at the water of the pond. I didn't see anything and started back for the car. Then I heard Ron say, "There it is," as if there was something we could shoot. It turned out to be a "teal" which is a very small duck. It was not big enough to waste a shot on! But the spotter, Ron, of this "monster duck that ate Topeka" fired his shotgun into the water. Then he started stepping back and firing. Did I mention that we had been drinking and Ron was no beginner in doing so!

Well, on the third shot he hit the guard rail flush. The small shot (bird shot not buckshot) hit the guard rail and bounced straight into another member (not Phil or me) but Richard Freeman! He got pellets up his side! I had dove back into the back seat of the car. I was getting pretty good at this diving out of danger thing! The only move to be made after this was to get Richard to an emergency room to get the pellets removed and getting that iodine, the yellow stuff, wiped all over Richard's side! We had put the shotguns in the trunk, still loaded, and I guess we forgot about them. Maybe too much beer? All of these mistakes were adding up! Stage one is over! Stage two of this Phil story is coming!

A few days later Mike Teter, aka Mike, and I, aka, Moochie, headed in to Wichita to do a little drinking and girl watching. We stopped at the "Roaring 60s" first and ran into Dennis Mitchell, another classmate. He was sitting watching one of the girls, Connie, who was one of our favorite dancers, dance. Dennis had his stack of quarters stacked in front of him. This was Dennis with his limit in quarters and how much he was not only going to spend but also how much he was going to drink. Draft beer was a quarter for an eleven ounce glass. As we sat there, we noticed more Goddard guys coming in and joining us. Phil, Richard, and, one we hadn't seen for a while, Kenny Allen. After a few beers we decided to do some bar hopping, and all of us climbed into Phil's car. Leaving the "Roaring 60s" and heading for the "Recess Lounge."

Well the "Recess" was dead, so we argued about our next stop. We decided on the "Playpen" on North Amidon. But before we left the Recess, one of our guys must have thought a rack of pool balls would look good on the wall of his apartment, so he procured (stole) them. Beer does strange things to people. It wasn't Phil, or Dennis, or Mike, or Moochie, but we were definitely with whoever did! As it became a part of Phil's car floor, especially under the trio's feet on the back seat: Dennis, Mike aka "Mike," and I aka "Moochie."

At the "Playpen," we evidently were going to stay a little while, as we ordered three pitchers with six glasses. I went to the bathroom, and when I came out the group said we were leaving. I asked, "What do we do with the beer?" We still had a couple of pitchers with beer in them and some nearly full glasses and I didn't want to leave, especially with one of our favorite dancers, Nikki, doing her turn of dancing! Somebody in the group said, "Bring them!" So we did! So with a couple of pitchers and some glasses filled with beer, we headed for the door. This time there were no innocents among the group as I joined the lawbreakers carrying my glass of beer out the door! Now we had paid for the beer but not for the pitchers and glasses. So if we were caught, we would be going to jail for a couple of glass pitchers and glasses; beer can make people stupid! Oh, and a rack of pool balls; beer can be dangerous when consumed in large quantities!

We got through the door without being stopped by anyone. This might have been a common occurrence at a bar. Maybe the hassling of good customers over something so minor might be bad for business. We were good customers, except when in a large group! We had spent many nights at the "Playpen" in small, two or three person groups, watching the girls in bikinis dance; okay, watching Nikki dance and obeying the common sense bar rules!

Oops, where were we, oh yeah, we arrived at Phil's car parked in the front of the bar; all of which was about three cars from the Playpen's door! We all got in the car except Richard who stood beside the car with Phil's car door open. Richard was arguing with a group of guys in the parking lot. Phil kept yelling at Richard to get into the car. Richard kept standing and yelling at the other group, so Phil must have thought Richard must need a small reminder! So he put the car in reverse and started the car slowly backward so Richard might get the hint while yelling, "Richard, we're leaving, get into the car." The only problem with Phil's action was the fact that the open door caught on the bumper of the car next to us! Richard finally got Phil's hint and got into the car pulling the door forcibly closed, springing the door.

With Richard back inside Phil's slightly damaged car, we left the "Playpen." As we left, I noticed another car pulled out right behind us. It seemed its driver was coughing into his hand as his car passed under a street light. The car was unmistakable in its appearance; it was a white Volkswagen! As it passed under another street light, it seemed the driver was still coughing into his hand. It didn't take a rocket scientist to guess he wasn't coughing into his hand; he was speaking into a radio in his hand!

We weren't sure who was in that VW bug, but surely we can outrun a "bug!" "Step on it, Phil!" As the members of group started giving conflicting ideas of how to do this, the "bug" passed under another street light on a turn, and on the side of the "bug" were letters "KFDI!" We were being chased by the "KFDI Eye on the Street," Jim Setters. "Faster Phil." The order came from somewhere in the car! Then the idea came. "Let's lose him on the bypass!" Then a song started playing in Moochie's head, "Beep, beep. Beep, beep, his horn went beep, beep, beep . . . the little Nash Rambler stayed right behind . . ." Not the "Playmates" again . . . Why . . . oh why, does this keep happening to Moochie?

Knock it off, brain, we're busy here! We are now on Central Avenue heading west toward freedom and the bypass! Just before reaching the bypass, the order came from somewhere in the car, "Turn left right up here." So Phil turned just before the bypass on to what we called the "electric works" road . . . The "electric works" was a huge bunch of transformers that supplied all the electricity for the world . . . Okay, how about for the west side of Wichita then? Hey geniuses with all of your help we are heading toward a "dead end." I knew both Mike and Moochie knew this, but who'd believe us or even listen to us. We were the youngest in the car; we were in the back seat, no sense even trying now.

The "cars," yes CARS, chasing us were now not just a lonesome "VW bug," but cars with flashing red lights. Now, most of the group was probably very disappointed at this development. But it might have been what saved everyone from death that night! If Phil's car could have got on the bypass, it would not have been a case of outrunning a "bug." Police cars are not slow; and with all the voices screaming "Faster Phil, faster . . ." now I could hear Mike's thoughts entering Moochie's . . . cue the music, Mooch . . . "So I pulled around and there we were . . . dead man's curve . . ." "That's Jan and Dean and their monster hit" came the DJ's voice in Moochie's head . . . "Dead Man's Curve!" Shut up brains! "Won't come back from dead man's curve . . ." SHUT UP!

Now on our way to the "dead end" (does anyone else notice how many times the word "dead" appears, Nostradamus?), there was a scramble to get the evidence of our nightly activities deposited elsewhere! So pitchers, glasses, and pool balls found a home outside of Phil's car! Would that have been "destroying of evidence" or "littering" or both? Probably both! I don't know if all the pool balls made it out, but later that would turn out to be the least of our problems. We had another problem that we had forgotten about: the loaded shotguns in the trunk! Could anything else show up on this ill-fated trip to drink beer? Oh yeah, how about the sawed-off twelve gauge Phil kept under his seat! Phil had made it into a twelve-gauge pistol shotgun! "Went to a party at the county jail . . ." not you too, Elvis! No time to "rock" now! Get out of Moochie's head! The sawing off of the twelve-gauge shotgun is and was a federal crime not local!

With the entire Wichita police force coming down the electric works road, we now had no chance! Our problem then was to hope the police cars didn't have an accident getting to their spots on this "monster bust!" How much do police cars cost? As our last effort to avoid capture, Phil drove around "The Last House on the Left" dead end (where does this stuff come from, brain? Yeah I do know . . . that vault of late night horror movies in Moochie's head)! How much does repairing of the side yard, back yard, and the other side yard where we gave up cost?

We sat and waited for instructions from our captors, the Wichita Police Force. They came up on all sides with guns drawn! Makes one wonder how the "Eye on the Streets," Jim Setters, described the perpetrators of the crime spree he had personally stopped in protecting the citizens of Wichita! "Out of the car; keep your hands where we can see them," came the order from one of "Wichita's Finest!" Which brought an "I can't" reply from Richard as his exit from the car was blocked by the sprung door. With what looked to be a bunch of very serious and very nervous, police officers, I thought it might not be smart "to be short in answering the order, Richard!" But no shots were fired, and after everyone was outside of the car it seemed to lessen the tension.

Until, that is, the sawed-off twelve gauge was found under Phil's seat! Now when the trunk was opened and the loaded shotguns were discovered in it, the tension returned! Although we knew we weren't the new Jesse James gang, the officers didn't. They loaded us into police cars to transport us to the jail.

Dennis and I were in the back, but when Mike was told to get in with us, he complained with his prosthesis; he couldn't get in to that tight of place. The officer then relented and told Mike to sit up front with him. When Mike opened the door, he stared at the briefcase on the front seat. The officer told Mike to just move it! So Mike, knowing how much room he needed to get in, took the briefcase and tossed it out beside the police car and did his entry on to the front seat. The officer was shocked how "cocky" these "perps" were. But after Mike showed how he had to enter the car, I think the officer understood it wasn't being "cocky" but reality for a double amputee. The officer picked up his briefcase and handed it to Mike who put it on his lap, and we started the journey to the police station.

The Wichita Police Department decided to let Mike, Dennis, and I post our own bail of $0.75! It was probably an amount to cover the paperwork as we three were never charged. Phil was toast, as the sawed-off shotgun was a federal crime. Kenny was charged because he had a pint of liquor on his person, he was nineteen, and not yet legal. By that, I mean stuffed down his pants. I think Richard was held as he was the most belligerent, or maybe he might have been charged with resisting arrest as he had said "I can't" when ordered to get out of the car.

After posting our "get out of jail" card, not free, but of seventy-five cents each, Mike, Dennis, and I were left with a long walk back to our cars still at the Roaring 60s. Lucky for us, a Goddard girl, Donna Carlson, saw us and gave us a lift back to the start of this strange night! Dennis went home. But Mike and I decided to put together a plan to get Phil, Kenny, and Richard free! We went to the Outer Limits to think. Once there, we kind of forgot, so the ones in jail would have to stay in jail, as when we started drinking beer and, as it has already been demonstrated, that all sense leaves after beer takes hold!

Richard and Kenny were released on bail the next day. Phil, who was facing more serious charges, took a little longer. Phil who was in the Marine Reserves ended up with his status changed to active. Not certain of the time line, but Phil was going to be taking a trip to Vietnam, just in time for the Tet Offensive. A well-hidden fact of the court system at this time, many young men were "encouraged" to join the military instead of facing jail time. *The Dirty Dozen*? A movie from that time but was set in WWII. Funny how our court system works! But Phil would return, and he would be a little older and a lot WISER!

Now there are many more stories of "Phil," as like I noted that just about all who knew Phil had at least one!

We might have to take a clue (oh no, not clue again), from the prison inmates' story and just use numbers or code words to signify which "remember when Phil" story we're telling! Jerry's antics will tell us if "that's a good one!" . . . or if the teller needs to work on his delivery!

# The Empty Chair

# Moochie Knowles

*Another name it could be called would be*
*"My Friend Mike"'*

I was the embodiment of the term "baby boomer." I was a child of the "1950s." Catching a very small piece of the "1940s" but experiencing every exciting minute of the "1950s."

Well, most likely every other "1950s" person would exclaim, "What?" after hearing me describe the "1950s" as being exciting. Well, I could debate with them as we did watch TV move from "tomorrow" right into our living rooms, first with one "exciting" channel and growing to three by the end of the decade.

Okay, that might have been the only "exciting" new thing for us kids to marvel over, but if your Mom was like mine, there were always books to read. Any whining about "but there's nothing to do" always brought a standard answer, "Get a book and READ!" So, Huck Finn and Tom Sawyer, Butch and Sundance, Frank and Jesse, and many others and their adventures entered my life.

My mother was an avid reader. If she ate like she read, she would have been confined to her bedroom, as she would not have fit through the door. She would devour magazines as soon as they arrived and then return to her staple of books. It seemed like the magazines were her dessert, but books were her "meat and potatoes."

Well, among her "desserts" was *Reader's Digest*, and it became mine as well. The *Reader's Digest* condensed version cut every story down to the "real story" without leaving out anything, it seemed. There were sections in every *Reader's Digest* that were in every issue. One of my favorites was "my most unforgettable person."

Well, after sixty plus years, and the elimination of a candidate that I might be partial to (my Mom), I think . . . no change that to I KNOW who would be my most unforgettable person . . . Mike Herndon.

Now, Mike was always a great friend. We were classmates at Goddard back before it became the monster it is now. We had forty-six graduates in our class. Everybody knew everybody.

Mike was our leader! He was the quarterback who led our football team; he was the toughness of our basketball team that carried us within a whisker's breath of a state championship. He was also one of the top pole vaulters in the state. He also never punched anybody that didn't deserve it.

None of that is why he is my most unforgettable person, although if I said he didn't strut when he walked, it might say something about the character of this man. Few people in the history of our small school had the right to "strut." Mike could have, but he never did! He always was a teammate, a classmate, a regular guy, a class act!

What happened this past May and June woke me up to the type of person my friend Mike was! A small group of us "old men" play nickel, dime, and quarter poker every Wednesday from 1:00 to 4:00 p.m. It was never about the money one might lose; it was just the getting together of nine former Goddard graduates, five from our class of 1967. Much of the conversations start with the standard "how you doing?" followed by the standard reply, "Okay, how you doing?"

Now, the reason we started the Wednesday ritual was to spend as much time as we could with Mike. You see, Mike was dying, and all of us wanted to join his fight with cancer, as if our numbers could stop that killer.

During the last summer of 2011, Mike had confided that the doctors had said that if he stopped the chemo, he wouldn't make it to Christmas. He told them the chemo was making him so sick; he wasn't sure he wanted to live anyway. So Mike stopped the chemo. Our small group stumbled around trying to come up with something that might make Mike's last days at least more enjoyable than a big dose of chemo. David threw out, "Why don't we just pick a day and play poker just like we did when we were kids?" It was obvious with everyone that this was the answer! This was going to be our gift to Mike to show him how much we loved him; little did we know that Mike had a gift for us!

The gift that Mike had for our group (and especially for me) had its start on the first Wednesday in May. We were holding our usual Wednesday poker game, and like all of our poker days, the participants mill around talking after it. I had been taking a cane with me for the last two weeks. Never one to beat around the bush, Jerry told me to show him the reason I had been whining for the last two weeks. Jerry didn't take to "wusses" real well, and he wanted to see the proof that I was hurting. As I took my sock off my right foot, Jerry winced and went silent for the first time in my fifty plus years of knowing him. David came to Jerry's rescue and said, "Mooch, you do know that they cut things like that off." By the time I got home, both my boys had been alerted to the fact that they were either taking me to the emergency center at Via Christi or the group would. My sons heeded the warning, and soon we were in the emergency center.

Things went fast and furious that first week, with me seeing four separate doctors. Mike took charge of our little band. We saw each doctor as a group with Alan pushing the wheelchair, Steeby taking notes, and Mike asking all types of great medical questions. Sometimes it seemed Mike was just as knowledgeable as the doctor. I just sat in the wheelchair, nodding with one eye always on Mike to see which way the nod should go.

After a couple of meeting with doctors, Mike told me he had been very tired. He almost didn't make that morning's meeting. He said Peg had to drag him out of bed and dress him. I asked him to at least take a break to get his strength back, as Alan had already told me that if Mike wanted a break, he could "pick up the ball and run with it." Mike said to keep Alan as a backup in case he couldn't make it.

The next morning Mike drove up my driveway at 6:00 a.m. Alan's offer had soundly been squashed. It was going to be Mike's ball to carry to the goal line.

Something he was great at as our quarterback in high school and even more so as our leader in life.

After the decision on amputation was made, Mike called a meeting. It was more like a huddle with him calling the play. At the meeting Mike told us he had a group ready to come in and clean my house from top to bottom! And also do a Clorox scrub to prevent me getting my leg infected. He said that few people die from the procedure, but many die from the wound getting infected. He also dictated the job of scrubbing down everything in my hospital room after the surgery to the group and especially my sons who would be visiting often.

At the end of the meeting, Mike posed his last question. Who I wanted to take me to the hospital the day of the surgery? I put my hand on Mike's and said quietly, "I want Mike to give me that ride to the hospital." Mike's shoulders had kind of slumped after asking that last question, but it seemed the shoulders raised back up after I answered. It was then that I finally grasped the concept of Love; every ounce of Mike's being was concentrated toward carrying me. He was dying quickly, and his concern for me getting through my ordeal was first and foremost on his mind and heart.

The day for the trip to the hospital came. Mike, as usual, was 15 minutes early. Alan arrived shortly after. We were always a group. It was the one-for-all, all-for-one-type thing. When we arrived at the hospital, Steeby was manning two wheelchairs. I guess if you have Dave standing behind you, everything is there for the taking.

The surgery went great! Dr. Pollock is a great surgeon and doctor, even if he calls himself just a carpenter. He passed the Mike test with a perfect score, and that was good enough for me!

The next period where I went from one hospital room to the Rehab Center was kind of blurry. I remember learning how to use a walker and the tricks of using a wheelchair. But for most of the days, I was in a drug-induced fog.

After I had mastered all the things they said I had to master, I was sure of my release date. Monday, June 18th. That date was going to get some altering. It was on Tuesday, June 12th, that Peg called to apologize for Mike and her not coming up the last few days. Peg confided that Mike wasn't doing that well. In the tone of her voice, I think I heard her cry, "Hurry Moochie, Mike has to see you and know you're alright again. He may not last till next Wednesday."

I don't know where I got the guts, but I immediately went down to the nurse's station and told them I needed about five hours off tomorrow. They replied that they didn't believe Medicare allowed that. I explained my situation in detail . . . They replied with the same answer . . . I could see this was getting nowhere . . . I asked to see someone who might have the power to at least work on the details of my leaving!

Yes, "my leaving," I was leaving for at least five hours on Wednesday with the staff's help or without it. It was their choice. When I said those words, the sound in my head sounded more like Mike's confident in control voice rather than my pleading stammering whine.

Like my heroes of fact and fiction, I set the wheels in motion of my leaving. I had called Sundance (Steeby) earlier. On the second call, he said he and Butch (Rob) would be at the lunch room at noon. Butch and Sundance were right on time, arriving at noon. Dr. Brown, however, was still busy getting all my scripts and paperwork done to satisfy Medicare. The only way I could do this was to be released from the Rehab Center and turned over to Home Health. The physical trainers ran me through all the things that I needed to be able to handle being at home with no backup. Each PT signed me off when I had completed their task. At a little after 1:00 p.m., we made our break, with the entire staff at Wesley Rehab Center in collusion with the "Wild Bunch." I know Mike smiled at all of our antics that we told him of our escape that Wednesday.

When we arrived at Mike's house, Mike responded to our successful break with one hand raised in a fist. Sundance rolled my wheelchair over next to Mike's so Mike and I could do a fist bump; it would be our last.

Mike Herndon passed away the following Sunday, June 17th, 2012; it was fitting that it was Father's Day. Mike's loving, wonderful wife, his five grown-up kids, and his three grandchildren were with him that day. Mike's Mom and Dad were only a few miles away, as were his sister and two brothers. Maybe that was his last play call, a quarterback keeper. We all know he crossed the goal line. I can only hope that my last days are as well planned.

Mike really deserved the term "most unforgettable person." At least for the poker gang (Steeby, David, Jerry, and Moochie from the 1967 class; Alan, Rob, and Ted from the 1968 class; and Ray from the 1965 class), the "most unforgettable person" is an understatement.

Mike's chair is still sitting empty. How can you fill it? The shoes are just too big.

# Moochie's Victories and Defeats

# *Chapter 1*

## Poems, Prayers, the Date, and Denver

How about a change in category? How about Moochie not only thinking, writing, or speaking in Moochie but also in Moochie's writing poems? Now that is something that very, and Moochie really means very, few knew about . . . like nobody! This one is entitled as follows:

A Dreamer
Steve or "Moochie" Knowles

A dreamer I am
And a dreamer I will always be
But without the dreamers
What a boring world this would be

For who would tell the child
Covered in mud from head to toe
That mud pies are all right
If they are baked real slow

And who would watch the stars
And while wondering at the sight
Ask God the questions
That troubles us on dark and starless nights

And who would protect the children
From fools who can never see
Fools who speak of ifs, can'ts, and should haves
And kill dreams before they can ever be

And who will name the clouds
As they change from face to face
Who else has time for things like this
As everyone else races from place to place

And who will dream the dreams
And dream of things that can never be
And with the innocence of a child
Make the impossible become reality

You see I am a dreamer
And I have a big job to do
I could use some help
How about you?

This was written in Moochie's sophomore year in high school. Do you know what it would have done to both Moochie's and my image if it would have gotten out then?

This next one is a pep talk that I used to devalue my (Moochie's) weaknesses and to hopefully move forward. It was written in Moochie's junior year to give Moochie and myself confidence in establishing relationships. It didn't work!

Hopes and Dreams
Steve (Moochie) Knowles

As you travel down life's twisting roads
Take with you only what you need
Those you love, never travel alone
And your hopes and dreams, never travel without them

Share your hopes and dreams with those you love
Share their hopes and dreams as well
Teach those you love the value of what you're giving
Know the value of what you're receiving

Hold theirs close to you with love and care
Pray they will hold yours in the same way
Help them as they reach for theirs
Hope they will help you as you reach for yours

Never kill a hope left in your care
And never let a dream die because of you
Never let your hopes starve; feed them regularly
And never let your dreams die from neglect; visit them often
Carry these with you as you walk down life's road
And they will carry you over the rocks put in your way
Hold on tightly to your hopes and dreams
And remember life is only over when
you can't dream anymore

High school ended on a low in my life, total embarrassment because of a date that I bombed. I will not say anymore if the lady wishes she can. She has no blame; all blame is mine alone. She will always be my dream girl. I never really knew her, but the vision of her I carried in my mind was very beautiful.

Two Nice People
Steve "Moochie" Knowles

Two paths running parallel suddenly twist and cross
Two people are caught in the situation
they have been tossed
So two people stand and stare
While wondering what brought the other one there

Two people wondering what to say
While wishing the other would start the play
Two people pondering what to do
So unable to find the courage to
utter a simple word or two

Two people wanting so desperately
to participate in the dance
Yet too afraid to take the chance
So two people turn and walk away
While thinking about what they wanted to say

Just two people not wanting to be hurt once again
Making excuses for their failure to begin
Two people deciding it wouldn't be nice to intrude
It wouldn't be polite. In fact, it just might be very rude
So two people prove they are so very polite
So very polite and so miserably nice

After the date, I wanted to hide; I wanted to die! I wanted to go as far away as I could to not face my shortcomings. I don't know if I wrote this to her to ask for forgiveness or for me to understand "it." But it was, and is my curse.

My Curse
Steve (Moochie) Knowles

Being able to write my thoughts and feelings
Yet never being able to say them
Like a mute, having to use sign language
Seeing beauty but having no voice
Never being able to express appreciation for the sight
Feeling wonderful affections
Silenced by the fear of ignorant utterances
Hopes and dreams
Being defined and interpreted by miss said thoughts
Being misunderstood by jumbled words and phrases
This is my curse

I had a serious mishap on my job during the last week before college started. I was running the "hot tar pot," melting the tar to waterproof a basement. When I got the tar melted, the next part of my job was to deliver it by carrying it in five-gallon buckets to the basement about fifty feet away. It was going to be my last duty, as I was starting college the next week. I got careless, as I wanted to get it done and go home!

All around a basement at this stage are the piles of dirt that came out of the "dig" for the basement. Many places it is just loose dirt. I ran when I should have walked. I guess my mind wasn't on what it should have been. I stepped on the loose dirt, and it slid under my feet. I went down to my knees. As that happened, the bucket hit the ground, and my hand and left arm found out what five hundred-degree tar feels like up close and personal like! It ended up costing me starting my first semester when everybody else started. It also meant skin grafts about every six months. It was just one depressing thing after another.

I was also used as an example for the bill that became law about having to be eighteen to work in dangerous jobs. I was seventeen and had worked in these so-called dangerous jobs for three years. I just got careless. It was my last day of work before starting college and more than anything else that was the reason!

I ended up not writing another line, another poem, for the next six years. I moved five hundred miles away, which started the "Mike and Moochie" chapters and story. I decided an adventure was what I needed. It was a good move; I was able to start all over with new friends. After a lot of great times with mostly new friends, unfortunately my life took a detour into a world I had never known, before: the worlds of jails and probation officers, also detailed in the "Mike and Moochie" story. Finally I started back. I met a young beautiful girl after the probation period, and she chased me instead of the other way around. I got married, and I was happy for a while. I was happy enough to return to writing poems.

This next poem deals with how and why of "Moochie Thinking Moochie." And it is a return to writing in kind of a humorous way. It is Moochie in the mid-1970s. It was kind of inspired by a road sign in the mountains west of Denver.

People with Rocks Rolling Inside Their Heads
Definitely by "Moochie"

There seems to be so many of them
And so few of us
I often wonder which way is best
Ours or the people with rocks rolling inside their heads

Sometimes I do find myself wanting to interfere
Wanting to tell everybody else how to live
Then I hear what sounds like thunder
Could it be that I also have rocks rolling inside my head?

For what can be written
Can also be said
But can it be understood by people
Hearing only the thunder of rocks
rolling inside their heads

So do we waste our paper?
Do we waste our breath?
On people who only listen
To the sound of rocks rolling inside their heads

So we do not give advice
For what good would it do?
To force our opinion on others
Like the people with the sound of rocks
rolling inside their heads do!

So we must be on guard
For no one is immune
To the "foot IN mouth" disease
Brought on by the thunder of rocks
rolling inside an empty head

There are signs beside the highways in the Rocky Mountains of Colorado that warn "Beware of Falling Rocks." I always thought that was truly a danger for people who should be wary of the rocks that constantly roll inside their heads! In some places marbles are substituted for the rocks! "Have you lost your marbles," get it! Driving through the mountains, I was an adult; I was tall!

This next poem is about . . .

Being Small
By Moochie

I saw things differently when I was small
But now I am tall
I did not worry about things when I was small
I knew someone would take care of me

Someone who was tall
Someone who truly loved me even though I was small
Someone who proved it with each and every day
Someone who could make all the dark clouds go away

I believed in wondrous things when I was small
But now I am not sure I believe in anything at all
When I saw a beautiful butterfly take flight
I watched in wonder at the sight
Now I wonder if butterflies should exist at all
It sure is sad being tall

Big Guy, Little Guy
Steve (Moochie) Knowles

I went to see who I was
I looked in the mirror
I saw a man
I saw him change
I saw him become a little boy

I watched him cry when he was hurt
I watched him beam with pride
When people would talk about him
I watch him play
He would always play by the rules
He could do nothing else
He was told to always be fair
He was not ready for the real world
He was not raised that way
He was told to always look for the good in people
He was told to always treat people the
way he wanted to be treated
He always did as he was told
He was an easy mark
He wanted to believe in the good in people
He could only see the good in people
Never the bad
He could not admit that people were
less than what he was taught
He was an easy mark
He could be used, taken advantage of
He got used to being used
He was happy to be of service
Then I saw him change back
The man was no different

Sometimes That's The Fun
Steve (Moochie) Knowles

Sometimes it's not the event

It's the dream of the event
Sometimes it's not the trip
It's the planning of the trip

So dream that dream
And plan that trip
You can go there now in your mind
Later you can go there in person

Freedom is just a state of mind
You can go anywhere you want
You have only one restriction
The restriction of how well you can dream

Sometime you may really go there
But don't be surprised if you're disappointed
Places can never match the dream
The dream of the way they are in your mind

So keep dreaming the dreams
Keep planning the trips
Don't be discouraged if you never go
Just start planning again, because sometimes that's the fun

# Chapter 2

# Tragedy and Friends

The middle 1970s brought happy times and sad ones too. The beautiful girl I married became with child shortly after our marriage vows were spoken. I was very happy with anticipation of a complete family with the announcement of my wife's new condition! My wife was even more beautiful than ever during the months of carrying our child. I did have to watch my sense of humor as she didn't see herself as beautiful during that time. Her emotions would swing wildly from happiness into depression, sometimes in minutes.

To me everything was going great! We found out it was a girl so we discussed what name we would give our wonderful daughter. We settled on Jennifer, the name with built-in shorts: Jenny or Jen! It seemed everybody wanted to hold a baby shower in anticipation of Jen! I was on top of the world. Hurry up Jen, get here, and the world will be right. My beautiful wife and Jen had entered their final week, together that is! Things could not get any more perfect . . .

I should have stayed home that week, but we both had our eyes fixed on our goals. We were going to need every dollar we could come up with as we didn't carry maternity insurance, but we could pay that off very easily in a couple months, we thought. As long as I continued working that is.

My wife got antsy one day during that week and took the car out for a drive. She said she never saw the Cadillac. With everything on her mind, that was very understandable after nearly nine months of carrying our bundle of joy. But a Volkswagen is no match for a Cadillac. Our happy world changed into a tragic world. A classmate of mine, Jim Rooks, happened to be the first on the scene and without him getting her out of the car and stopping the bleeding I might have lost both my wife and Jen. We did lose Jen, and my wife spent the next eight days in intensive care and then three more weeks in the hospital. She had a broken hip and had internal injuries that had caused Jen's death. But my wife lived!

During those weeks, I only left the hospital to shower and shave, usually only when a close friend or relative came up and took over my watch. But I also had one other thing I had to do. At a very private graveside service I said good-bye to Jennifer.

When my wife was in intensive care, I slept in a chair in the waiting room. After she was moved to a hospital room, I slept in a chair in her room. When I wasn't sleeping, I sat thinking about her in that bed. There was nothing to do but be there when she woke up. That was my life at that time. I couldn't go to work; I couldn't function until I knew she was going to "make it" back from that world she was in. I went through a lot of self-blaming periods while I sat thinking, *If only I had . . .*

Finally, after a month I was able to take her home in a wheelchair. The initial prognosis was not good. She may never walk again, and if she did, she would always need a cane. My classmate, Mike Teter, and his wife, Betty, offered their home for my wife to recover in. Betty took over the caring for my wife during the day while I worked. That's what friends do! I was very thankful for them being my friends. Friends not only offer, but they insist on the giving of their help.

My wife showed her determination, and I became very happy and proud of her desire to prove those doctors wrong. With every step she took, she was proclaiming that she was going to walk again and without a cane! She was amazing in her battle! The doctors also said that she might not be able and probably should not have children, as it could be dangerous to her. Like her battle of proving the doctors wrong about her walking again, she fought the odds! She was not going to let anything deter her from the life we had talked about when Jen was at the center of our hopes and dreams! Two years later we welcomed the first of two miracles into our family; Johnathon Robert Knowles was name of the first miracle. The second miracle was born three years later when Marc Allen Knowles joined the family! Both had to be delivered by C-section, but they were born and healthy! We were buried in debt from the accident and two children born without insurance as my wife could not be insured. But my wife was walking and the world was right again, and we were happy!

# Chapter 3

## Texas, Challenges, and Youth Baseball

The 1970s ended and the 1980s began. With the birth of my second son, the 1980s started on a high note. Who would have thought something that started so brightly would turn so dark by the end of the 1980s? We had moved to Texas in 1985 to get a new start. Texas was booming in the home-building business, and I was a carpenter. Wichita was going through a downturn. It might have been my vagabond nature or just going to where the work was but we were in Texas!

We ended up settling in Euless, Texas, a suburb halfway between Dallas and Fort Worth. I quickly got a job with a construction company as a framing carpenter. The help wanted ad in the paper said the job paid $10 dollars an hour for experienced carpenters. I told the man hiring that I would work for that for one week. I did have a number in my head that was more than $10 an hour.

He took the challenge, and I went to work. The job foreman assigned me to frame, what he said was, a fancy drop ceiling. He must have figured it would take all day as he went back to what he was doing, leaving me to figure it out on my own. For me there was no figuring it out. It was a simple drop ceiling with the sides angled up to flat ceiling! I finished it in about two hours and went to find the foreman.

The foreman was working on the roof at the back of this "monster house." In Texas all things are bigger, and this house was not the exception but the norm! I told him that I had finished the job and asked, "What do you want me to do next?" As he climbed down from the roof, I thought I heard him mutter, "Ain't no . . . way," with an explicit adjective in the middle. I think he was thinking about firing me for interrupting him while he was all the way up to the top of this "monster" and evidently (to him) difficult house! We finally reached the room (things are always bigger in Texas), with the drop ceiling. He was quiet as he studied how it was done. After standing there for what seemed like an hour, he told me to follow him. He took me to three more rooms that needed the same drop-type ceiling. He then told me nobody before had done what he called a "splay ceiling" in one day, let alone in two hours. He even assigned a "gopher" to help me! "Gopher," or "Go-fer," is a term in construction for a laborer whose job is to go-for whatever the carpenter needs. I didn't need one, but it was a sign of respect!

The foreman's name was Tom. The next day, in an early morning conversation, I would return the respect he had given me the first day. I didn't know what the traffic would be like in getting to the house we were framing, and I tried always to be early. So I was a half hour early. Tom showed up just a few minutes later. We had that showing up early thing in common. I had always used this time as a way to map out what I wanted to get done. This day, it gave me a chance to talk personally to Tom without his crew around. We talked, and he admitted he was great on building floors and walls but roofs were a totally different thing. He had trouble with roof framing. I said, "Tom, roofs are my strong point, and I can help you there." There was no need to talk about how we should respect each other. In the way I had showed up early and discussed things with no one else around demonstrated my respect for him, so we got along great!

The first week went by, and the owner of the company made a special trip just to discuss my pay, another sign of respect. The topic, my pay, was handled also with respect. He said, "I can't pay you what you're worth on this house, but if you'll stay with us, I will put together a new crew for you." With the way it was handled, I said, "Okay, I'll do it."

One thing I had never done was building a circular stairway. All of these monster homes, in the high dollar area that we were in, had a circular stairway that was the focal point of the entryway to each home. Tom had showed me the plans to the house we were framing that second day. There it was, what I had always wanted to build, a circular stairway! Tom told me they had a subcontractor come in and build it after we finished. I set my sights on changing that and started buying the books about building circular stairways. On the second house we did in Dallas, I convinced my boss I could build a circular stairway and DID!

It was one more check off on my personal "bucket" list. I did make an enemy though by doing it. The circular stairway subcontractor came to visit me after I finished the first one and offered me a job just building circular stairways. He said he had made $340,000 the year before, just building circular stairways (in 1985 dollars, in today's dollars, that would be close to $1.25 million). He offered me a job with his company at a substantial raise over what I was getting. I turned him down. One reason was I had given my word when I first started to my boss that I would stay with his company. The second was that I was infatuated with the total job of framing these, as Tom would say, monsters! Not just circular stairways, I wanted to build it all. It was a challenge!

For me, work was never about money. It was about accomplishing something. Too much Dad in me, I guess! Where I was, new accomplishments didn't happen just every week, month, or year, but sometimes every day! I was where I was meant to be; I loved it and the challenge of it. I'm sure I beamed when I told my wife what the "circular stairway subcontractor" offered and I turned down. I'm sure she didn't!

Later on at the company Christmas party she got to meet the two girls who worked in the company office. They told my wife of the changes in the company since I came to work. One girl even told of a time when I stopped by the office, three guys were there because their car had broken down right in front of the office. They had used the company phone to call for help. I picked up whatever I was there for and walked back to my truck. All the time thinking of the look the girl had given me. I took it as a look of fear and she was all alone, so I walked back into the office and told her I would stay until quitting time when she would lock the doors and go home. The guys left after their help arrived, and her fears faded. It may have been nothing, but she was very happy when I came back to the office that day!

There were other changes besides just caring about coworkers. The girls were getting paid every week, and the boss never missed a week in doing so. After I started working there, that is! In construction, it isn't unusual for the owner to get behind in the pay of the office help. Their stories of changes in the company were nice to hear, but, unfortunately, it might have just opened my wife's eyes to the pitfalls of working in construction, the "here today, gone tomorrow" of construction. It was the same in construction everywhere! It was the reason we moved to Texas!

My wife had also quickly found a job at a large corporation, Shed Spread, in their office. I was once again proud of her, and we were finding things looking up. We were still in huge debt from the wreck, but we were paying it off, maybe a little slower than the hospital and doctors wanted, but we were consistent in our payments.

In the summer, our boys wanted to play baseball, and I volunteered to help coach. I had done a lot of coaching youth baseball in Kansas. Soon I was able to show the head coach that I was more than just a Dad. He made me his assistant coach. Now, coaching youth baseball in Texas was different from what I had done in Kansas. There was a major league team headquartered just twenty miles south of us, the Texas Rangers. I went to the meeting they held for the youth coaches with a legal pad in hand. The drills these "professional baseball people" demonstrated were fantastic! I took a full ten pages of notes. I believed I was there for a reason! Oddly, I noticed I was the only one there that took notes. I guess everybody else had already gone through this before. But I doubt too many really had paid attention like I was doing that year!

John was an eight-year-old that first year in Texas. He made a major splash in that big pond his first year in Texas. Of course nobody in Tri-Cities Youth Baseball knew, at the beginning, who John or I was, but that would change, at least in John's case. John showed in the early practices he was one of the top players on the team. When league play started, John proved to be one of the best players in the league. He was maybe the top hitter in the Midget League that year, as well as being one of the top four pitchers. I say a definite number because I had never seen as many great youth pitchers in one place, and the top four were incredible, including John. By the end of the season I wasn't known as the assistant coach of the Dodgers, but I was known as John's Dad.

I loved being John's Dad. Because in my family every member gets credit for their achievements if done fairly or held responsible for their actions if done poorly or if considered bad! Bad could be just taking credit for someone else's achievements. So being called John's Dad was John being in the spotlight and being applauded for HIS achievements. It was not for being my son, which could cause those achievements to revert back giving the credit to me. It was just the way ownership was viewed in our family. But showing pride is considered great as long as it isn't taking credit, got that!

John was voted onto the All Star team unanimously! That team played in the best Midget League game I ever saw, but lost 1–0 to a Dallas team in the district playoffs. John had hit two screamers to centerfield in which the center fielder made great catches after he ran them down! These are eight-year-old boys; they are not supposed to be able to do that! During that game John and I witnessed the reverse of the practice of a father taking credit for his son's play! John's team's best pitcher ended up being listed as the losing pitcher in the game that day, not of his own accord but because of errors committed behind him.

After that heartbreaking loss, the pitcher was slowly walking, with his head down, to his Dad's truck when the Dad said, "Losers don't ride in my truck." Followed by, "Go ride with your mother!" Wow, his son had just pitched one of the best and most gritty pitching performances I had ever seen. And his Dad called him a loser! I was just a Dad just watching my son play, but I had been a coach and had seen the signs of injury before. And his son was hurting, not just mentally but also physically. He was also dying inside from his Dad's cruel words!

That pitcher was the top pitcher of the Midget League, and his Dad was the head coach of the All Star team. I guess the winning of the game was more important to the Dad, the coach, than even his son. I had watched the son during league twice and during the All Star games. In that last game he was showing signs of being overused! He was grimacing after every pitch and holding his arm abnormally after each pitch also. I went over and talked to his Dad and told him what I noticed. He blew me off saying his son was using that as an excuse and he did it all the time. To me, I had done everything I could do. I went back to my seat in the bleachers and sat down. Having pride in your son's play and accomplishments is one thing, but living through a son is very ugly to see. Taking credit for the accomplishments of the son is even worse and is the same as stealing from his son! It was in my family anyways!

In our league, known as Tri Cities, recruiting for the next year starts as soon as the previous season ends. All the coaches tried to steal John from his coach of the previous year. One of those coaches was the coach that told his son . . . "Losers don't ride in my truck. Go ride with your mother!" Both John and I said "NO"!

Now John was fantastic during his first year in Texas, but another kid was the story that year for me. Unlike the first example of what can be wrong in youth sports. This next example shows all the points of why baseball can be great for kids in more ways than just playing a game. It is about teaching for all the right reasons . . . and a mother's love!

I had a love for baseball as far back as I could remember. I always believed that it taught a lot of things that kids should learn, if only they are taught the right way. I think every coach, whether a volunteer or paid, should know how much impact they can make in the youth of our society. The things taught to the youth go beyond baseball. The big effect of teaching any type of youth sports go into the makeup of every kid you have taken the responsibility of coaching. One of the most important responsibilities of coaching young kids is the nurturing of their self-confidence in the things they do! Having confidence opens doors in their life; after all this game called baseball is just a memory from their childhood!

My favorite story of helping a kid develop self-confidence through his playing the game of baseball is "The Story of Andrew." This happened during my first few years of more than twenty-five years of coaching youth baseball. Whenever anybody asks, "Why would anyone devote so much time to coaching youth baseball?" I tell them "The Story of Andrew"; most then understand the "why."

It seems that every baseball team has at least one kid who is destined to be a project. A project is a kid who tries so very hard, but circumstances and sometimes just bad luck seemed to follow him, keeping him from achieving success. The other kids seem to achieve success without the desire that he had within himself. That was Andrew in 1986!

My heart went out to Andrew that year. I tried everything I could to help him overcome whatever was holding him back. With my son, John, on the same team, we would call Andrew whenever we went to the batting cages. Andrew really wanted to play baseball, and his mother encouraged him in his desire to do so. Andrew was a slightly built kid. Although John and Andrew were the same age, John outweighed Andrew by about twenty-five lbs. John did have other advantages over Andrew. This was Andrew's first year of playing baseball. John was in his third year, and I had coached him during those first two years, and I was the assistant coach of the team in this, John's third year.

Andrew had little confidence, but his desire carried him through those early practices and with the trips to the batting cages Andrew was showing a lot of improvement. The first league game brought a lot of anticipation for both Andrew and me. In that game we faced one of the hardest throwers in the league. But he was also wild. On Andrew's first plate appearance, he was hit and that pitcher threw very hard! After the tears subsided, the fear took over. That game Andrew got three more plate appearances. Andrew was nowhere near the plate as he left the batter's box just as soon as the pitcher started his windup. He struck out all three times as he did swing with every pitch as being in the batter's box was not where Andrew wanted to be! Since swinging at every pitch was the best way to get back to the safety of the dugout, Andrew took it.

So it could be called going back to the drawing board, but nothing in this could be called "back." This was a whole new situation, total fear!

But we did go back to work. This time, it was to get Andrew to stay in the batter's box. The only thing that could cure Andrew's fear was the excitement of Andrew hitting the baseball. The standard fix of teaching kids to overcome the fear of facing another kid's pitching was to put bats behind the feet. That did not work as Andrew would leave the box as soon as the pitcher started his windup, stepping over the bats. His mother and I took Andrew to the batting cages, once again, to work on his hitting. In fact, many times it was just her and Andrew at the batting cages. The only answer we could come up with was Andrew finding the magic feeling that comes from hitting a baseball. His mother's work with Andrew was special; she was always positive and patient with her encouragements. In the cages he was staying in the "box" and was hitting the ball. With all the hitting practice his swing had become flawless! So on a day in the middle of the season, since he had stopped "bailing out" in practice, we felt he was ready "to hit."

Andrew was facing the league's top pitcher, but that pitcher also had the best "control" in the league. This pitcher had thrown twenty-seven strikes out of twenty-eight pitches in the earlier game that season against us! I felt the matchup was perfect for Andrew. With his "perfect" swing and the pitcher's amazing control that was known by all in the league, I thought Andrew just might shock everybody that day with a hit, but at worst, I was sure he would hit the ball. As Andrew took his place in the batter's box on his first "at bat," not only Andrew's mother but I and every parent who had ringside seats to Andrew's battle all year held our breaths. And then it happened, no, not Andrew's hit but a different type of hit. The pitcher with the unbelievable control had a pitch "get away" and hit Andrew! Now what do we do? Andrew, once again, struck out every "at bat" following that with "one foot in the bucket" before the pitch was even made. He was out of the batter's box when the pitch was made. His mother and I were back to square one, as well as Andrew!

The battle started again; this time I was worried that Andrew might have lost his faith in his mother and me. We had been concentrating so much on getting him to stay in the box that we never told him how to avoid pitches that could hit him. We started all over again. His mother made the batting cages Andrew's second home! I had never seen a mother so dedicated. I had stressed what I thought was the importance of baseball in its effect on kids all through their lives. I could go into all those things, but having self-confidence was one of them, and Andrew did not have it. And with his experiences in his first year in baseball, he was not going to gain much in that first year. But his mother just would not quit.

So we had one half of a season to get Andrew a hit. Unfortunately neither I nor his mother could get in that batter's box. Andrew would have to do it! As the season wore on, Andrew had started at least staying in the batter's box, but he was way too anxious in the timing of his swing. He usually had his swing finished before the ball reached home plate. It seemed Andrew had overcome his fear of the baseball, but he still struck out every at bat. At first we were happy he was not stepping out of the "box," but it seemed like other problems were becoming evident. He wasn't just swinging too early, he was swinging at every pitch AND swinging too early! I wondered if Andrew might have developed a strategy to please his mother; was he closing his eyes and just swinging to keep his mother thinking he had conquered his fears? I tried to see if that were true, but if he was, I couldn't see it. I was in a quandary, I wanted him to be more selective in the pitches he swung at, but I didn't want him thinking too much and cutting down his aggressiveness.

The season came down to the last game. I really wanted Andrew to get his hit or at least hit the ball. He was the only kid that hadn't yet accomplished either. The team we faced that day was the team leading the league, and they had not one but two of the top pitchers. I almost said something to the other coach during our meeting at home plate. I was thinking about maybe asking him to tell his pitchers to ease up when Andrew came up. But I didn't! I knew later on somebody would eventually tell Andrew and destroy him with that news. So I put it in other hands and prayed. His mother and I had done everything we could do! I had tried every trick in my bag and still Andrew was hitless! I knew Andrew was probably playing his last game as he probably would not come out the next year.

Well, I resigned myself to my failure. Well, sometimes God must take in a little boy's baseball game. Either that or God wrote the script to the ending of a little boy's season! In Andrew's first at bat that day he swung at the ball on the first pitch as he had done before. But this time Andrew's bat connected solidly, and the ball flew over the left fielder's head! It could have been because this pitcher had a lot on his pitches, speed wise. It might have been because the batting cages that were like Andrew's second home threw at the same speed. I didn't care the reason! The ball went clear to the left field fence on a couple of hops. Andrew's first hit that season was a home run!

I'll never forget the look of pure joy on Andrew's face as he circled the bases. That look on Andrew's face made all the hours, that although frustrating most of the time, worth it! Later in that game Andrew drove another over the center fielder's head. They had even backed up after his first hit, but he beat them again for a double. It was like he was saying very loudly, "The first hit was not a fluke!" Then he did something I had never seen before; he pointed at me in the dugout, and he raised his hand and made a fist pump. He then swung his arm around to where his mother was and blew her a kiss!

Andrew did come out the next year. In fact he was the leadoff hitter, and my son John batted cleanup as they were once again teammates. I watched every game except those games that were played at the same time as my Euless Dodger's game in the Midget League. I think Andrew must have struck out at least once the next season, but it must have been in one of those conflicted games, because I never saw it! I did get to see the game that Andrew got four hits in . . . okay it was three hits as Andrew was the one who got hit on the fourth one. But after being hit, he dropped the bat and ran to first base . . . no crying . . . no tears . . . just a stern look toward the pitcher. Andrew had become what he dreamed of, a baseball player, and from his last game in Midget League he developed a reputation . . . Andrew Comes to HIT!

Marc was playing T-Ball that year, and my wife volunteered to help. Once again I was filled with pride for her doing this. We were getting to be among the community's finest citizens. I stayed the next year in Midget so I could coach Marc the year after. I was even interviewed by a Dallas paper with a headline "They come to hit!" That line explained my philosophy of coaching youth baseball. At seven to eight years, old kids should get the excitement in hitting a baseball. It should never be about winning at that age.

I told the kids if you can reach it, hit it! I even had the parents tell kids that did walk to say, "You'll hit it next time," and I told the parents that they should not applaud walks. In the game when I was interviewed we had sixteen hit balls, not always for hits, but many kids on our team got the excitement of hitting a baseball. The other team usually kept their bats on their shoulders as their coaches would criticize their kids for swinging at pitches outside the strike zone. They hit the baseball three times, but they won the game 16–10 as they had many walks. I think one of the parents had been behind the reporter just showing up looking for a "human interest story," and I guess the reporter thought it was interesting enough. The paper ran the story of the nut that coached the team: me!

I never got to coach Marc that next year. The Texas economy went into a tailspin, and I came back to Kansas to work with my brothers while the company in Dallas tried to find work for us. Our expenses in Texas were running well over $3000 a month. The only place I knew of to get that was back in Kansas, it was not going through a depression like the one that had hit Texas. So I started driving back to Texas every couple of weeks and giving my wife my checks. During that time, she had made the statement that I was the noblest person she had ever known, but she followed that with, "I just can't live like this anymore!" I didn't know how long this thought had been rolling inside her head.

It might have been about my having to be in Kansas. It might have been my attitude about work. In Kansas, I would be going back to subcontracting, where my concern would probably seem, to her, to be more about the employees welfare and not my family's. It could have been about the money that the circular staircase builder offered and I turned down. All those things might have signaled to her I was never going to change. But it was over. She wanted me out of her life! I guess our marriage was not as strong as I thought. But I didn't tell anyone about the failed marriage, and for a while and I kept giving my checks to her. At that time she was still my wife even if she didn't act like it. I felt I still had a responsibility for the family.

Once again I turned to music and Roy Orbison to understand what had just happened. This is *It's Over* written by Roy Orbison and Bill Dees.

It's Over

Your baby doesn't love you anymore
Golden days before they end
Whisper secrets to the wind
Your baby won't be near you anymore

Tender nights before they fly
Send falling stars that seem to cry
Your baby doesn't want you anymore
It's over

It breaks your heart in two
To know she's been untrue
But oh what will you do?
Then she says to you
There's someone new
We're through We're through
It's over. It's over. It's over

All the rainbows in the sky
Start to weep, then say goodbye
You won't be seeing rainbows anymore
Setting suns before they fall,
Echo to you that's all, that's all
But you'll see lonely sunsets after all
It's over It's over It's over It's over

The reasons might have really come down to this.
All through my life it can be pointed out by the words
in another song by Paul Simon . . . "I've built walls . . . A
fortress deep and mighty . . . That none may penetrate . . .
I have no need of friendship, friendship causes pain . . . It's
laughter and it's loving I disdain . . . I am a rock . . . I am
an island" "And a rock feels no pain . . . And an island never
cries." I guess the song *I Am a Rock* could describe me and
my beliefs perfectly. In fact, nothing describes my life as
completely . . . "Don't talk of love . . . But I've heard the
words before . . . It's sleeping in my memory . . . I won't
disturb the slumber of feelings that have died . . . If I never
loved I never would have cried . . ." And the last lines hit
me hard . . . "I have my books . . . And my poetry to pro-

tect me . . . I am shielded in my armor . . . Hiding in my room, safe within my womb . . . I touch no one and no one touches me . . . I am a rock . . . I am an island . . . And a rock feels no pain . . . And an island never cries." I don't know why I've always had trouble expressing that to people that I've love. But that's just me. A rock . . . An island.

# Chapter 4

## Divorce, Darkness, and Hospitals

Her announcement was followed by three days of almost endless tears for me. I tried not to let her see my tears, but she did. Then another blow: she was taking me off her employer's health insurance policy through her work. When she first started working, after the wreck, it was to get health insurance for the family. When she announced that I would no longer have health insurance, I didn't think it was a big deal. I had never used it, but I was going to find out almost immediately why it was so very important! Shortly after leaving, I wrote this poem. The next writings are from that period of self-doubt and very dark thoughts. They are only there because of a high school classmate's belief, Susan Shaw, that they may have some benefit to people going through the pain of divorce. I guess friends of fifty plus years are hard to shake. And after fifty plus years, these true friends know how to approach the pain of my shattered relationship and the broken heart left behind.

I Miss You
Steve (Moochie) Knowles

I miss you now more than you'll ever know
But I cannot change what has happened
Just as I know I cannot change you or your mind
Just as I cannot change the past
My heart cries
But no tears fall from my eyes
For no one must ever see
How much you mean to me

I Still Love You
Steve (Moochie) Knowles

To love her more than she'll ever know
To be adsorbed in thoughts of her
To hurt deeply yet returning just to be near her
Prolonging not postponing pain
Not wanting anything else
If all she has to give is pain
I'll accept what she gives
To be able to fly touching the candle's flame
Is better than being stuck in the wax below

I had moved in with Mike Teter, another friend and
classmate who had shared so many adventures with me.
He and his wife, Betty Jo, had cared for my wife after the
wreck. Their opinion of my wife took a nosedive espe-

cially after she took me off the health insurance. They both thought it was very spiteful of her to not wait until the divorce was final. Sometimes that hurt and anger also came out of me.

Betty Jo
Steve (Moochie) Knowles

The pieces of my life lay scattered all around me
All the memories, good and bad
All the fears, some imagined, some real
I hate to restrict your movements
But be careful where you step

You can't hurt her by stepping on
the pieces where you see her
But you can hurt me, thank you for caring
Thank you for gently picking up each piece
I know that inside some pieces are things
that she used to hurt you deeply
Yet you treat them with so much love and understanding

It would have been so easy for you to sweep
those pieces up, with contempt
No one would blame you
Others have done it
Yet you saw and understood my love for her
My view of her was seen through my love for her

Love, blind to all faults
Love, seeing only what it wanted to see
You made me understand that
You made me see her without destroying her
You knew all the pieces had to be
carefully put back in their place

Even ones with images distorted
You knew I needed all of them to rebuild
You knew I could never really hate her
Now that I can honestly see her, I can go on without her
I won't build a shrine for her and crawl inside it
But I can keep the good essence of
her inside me in memories
Thank you, Betty Jo

Once again I traveled into a "neverland" of
doubts and pain, lashing out I saw no escape.

Tell Me
Steve (Moochie) Knowles

What can you tell me?
What can you tell me of honor?
What do you know of honor?

Do you honor me with your presence?
Or do you curse me with your existence?
So, what can you tell me of honor?

What can you tell me of truth?
What do you know about truth? Was your life with
me filled with truth? Or was it dominated by deceit
and trickery? What can you tell me of truth?
What can you tell me of love?
Did you ever really love me?
Or are you only a receiver never a giver?
So, What can you tell me of love?

So what is it that you can tell me? Can you tell me
of things that you have no understanding of?
How?

Mike and Betty's basement became my home after leaving Texas. I had to have somewhere to live. Mike and Betty Jo said they wanted me to stay with them. I guess they were worried about my depression, probably with good cause! I wasn't very stable mentally. I was not eating very much. For the first time, since I was a freshman in high school, my weight dropped under 130 lbs!

I guess somebody had ratted on me to Mom; I think it was my brother, Chuck. During a depressive evening, which I was having a lot of, Mike Teter had called him. So I went to Mom and Dad's. I also had developed an abnormally swollen right leg. It was a great time to be without health insurance! So they called my family doctor, and he said to take me to the hospital in Kingman.

My family doctor there had some preliminary diagnosis of my illness. His initial diagnosis centered on my right leg that had swollen to a very noticeable size by this time.

His diagnosis was of a kidney infection. He also believed I had a blood clot in my leg that was also helping to cause the leg to swell. He was half right! They put me on blood thinners for the clot and antibiotics for the kidney infection.

I was also served my wife's "desire to divorce" me papers. A hospital is a very perfect setting to be served divorce papers. My wife called me complaining to me that her foster mother (my aunt) condemned her for the divorce. Her next statement is still confusing to me thirty years later. She defended her divorcing me by saying, "Don't they understand I'm doing this for the boys!" She followed that up saying that it took courage to do what she was doing! She was talking to me! It was like I was her only friend, not the one she was divorcing! This set off a lot of angry thoughts in my head. It was like a door, not being just closed, but slammed shut! Losing all hope, I wrote this.

Just Thoughts
Steve (Moochie)

She told me that it takes a lot of courage
to do what she had done
Yes it does, to rip a heart out and hold
it while it beats its last beat
To hold it in front of me and coldly smile
For how long does this torture go on?
The pain seems like the pulse of the heart
Hitting hard then fading only to return
Pain triggered by words; sometimes by actions

Words and actions seem rehearsed
Each one planted carefully for maximum torture
Each one carefully set then driven
home with intense pleasure
What did I fall madly in love with?
What type of devil am I facing?
I should be happy to be released from this
What I have to do will take a lot of courage
To walk away from her as I still loved
her with every beat of my heart

Every time I moved toward despising, loathing, and hating her, it seemed like after my expressing it, I went through a total reversal. No matter what, I still loved her an awful lot!

I Just Don't Cry Anymore
Steve (Moochie) Knowles

I still dream of you in the night
I still cry out for you in the darkness
I still reach out for you when I wake
But I just don't cry anymore

I still look for you in our favorite places
I still listen for your singing in our songs
I still think of your dance where we use to
But I just can't cry anymore

I still long to smell your fragrance
I still long to savor your essence
I still long for you, giggling and naked and so lovely
But I won't cry anymore

I still remember you with white puppies at your feet
I still watch for you in sunsets of purple and gold
I still search for you at the end of rainbows
But you won't see me cry anymore

But if you do, please turn away
Because tears just don't look good on me anymore

The reference to "white puppies at your feet" was because of a wedding present by a friend while we were on our honeymoon in Denver, Colorado. The present was a "pure-breed Samoyed" that a breeder friend of mine wanted us to have the "pick of the litter." Its name was Alisha Bacardi, officially, but we called her "Puppy." The white puppies, Alisha's brothers, and sisters seemed to have taken a "likin" to my beautiful wife instantly. It seemed they were all screaming for her to also take them home with us. White puppies at her feet! After my wife's wreck, my folks took Alisha home with them, as I was living in the hospital . . . waiting! On one of my parents' visits joining me on my vigil. My Mom tearfully told me how they had found Alisha laying beside the entrance of the fence into their front yard. She had been hit by a car or truck. She was still alive, but later at the vet she died from the internal injuries. So we not only lost Jennifer but also Alisha.

In my head I hear David's booming voice, "Moochie, what does that have to do with the price of rice in China?" Actually nothing big guy, but I loved that puppy that I first saw as a member of the gang of puppies around someone's feet. I also miss her, that puppy and the woman with those feet that the puppies gathered around that day long ago.

Sorry, back to the hospital. At this time the mobile CAT scan was doing its rounds through the smaller hospitals, and they ran me through it. The report was that I had cancer. In a weird way, that saved my life, because my current treatment would have killed me! It was that half-wrong thing that was getting ready to announce its presence, but not yet! My family doctor gave me the cancer speech, which would have caused any patient anguish and sorrow, but to me it was a way to exit from the scene. He had me transferred to a Wichita hospital that dealt with cancer cases.

There, the doctors did a biopsy to determine what stage the cancer was in. But there was one problem. They couldn't find the cancer. But they had kept running blood thinner into me to dissolve the clot. The doctors then started trying to find the mysterious disease that was killing me. They asked me some very interesting questions like, "Have you been out of the country in the last six months?" "Have you met anyone who had travelled out of the country or that was from another country?"

Wow, they didn't know what I had! I wondered if I was going to have a disease named after me! It sometimes seemed that they were waiting for me to die so they could find out why! They ran tests on everything, even a neurologist came in and asked me questions; he might have even ordered some tests. By this time I don't think they could keep track of all the tests they ordered. The circus seemed to have come to town!

My brother, Chuck, had heard enough theories and half-baked diagnoses that were really getting "out there!" Someone said he grabbed a doctor by his smock, which was later denied, but Chuck did agree with the term "getting their attention!" Chuck did say he very plainly said to get back to what they did know, "the swollen and getting more swollen leg!" Dag'nab'it Chuck, I had never had a circus built around me before! I was the "star attraction!" I was going to be owner of the next big disease; I was going to be as famous as Lou Gehrig! I was going to be dead, but I was going to be famous!

But it is amazing how the "hopes and dreams" of national recognition leave the room when common sense walks in. The doctors went back to doctoring and inserted a mini camera in my leg. The "blood clot" turned out to be an aneurism! And the kidney infection was getting to be a ball of infection the size of a softball! The potential cause of death had announced its presence! Now the problem became the blood thinners that I was on to dissolve the clot that wasn't there! An aneurism is one thing that has to be operated on to get it fixed before it blows.

But the doctors could not operate as I would die as any bleeding could not be stopped. I would bleed to death and die, "Moochie bleeding to death is already called dying!" Even when he wasn't around, I could hear David's booming voice in my head! The aneurism was showing signs that it was getting ready to blow and that would also kill me. They waited, they had stopped the injections of blood thinner, duh, and started injections to thicken the blood, double duh, but they continued waiting. It was a rush to beat the aneurism blowing and having the operation to fix the aneurism and remove the "ball of infection." And they waited . . . Who won? As I lived through, it could be said that I won. But did I? I figured the score was 0 for me and at least 3 for all those who were not me.

I was still in a hospital bed; I was still going through a divorce that I did not want, and I was getting farther into debt with each day spent in the hospital. Even though my brother Chuck kept saying I should sue for the circus of care I received, I could not. I still believed as a whole that the doctors had tried to save my life, and even though that was in doubt for a while, they did! I almost changed my mind one evening as I was recovering from the ordeal when one of the nurses wanted to get me prepped for a procedure the next morning. I told her I had not been informed of anything that I needed to be prepped for. She asked me, "Are you Mister Knowles?" I said yes. She then called me Alfred. Alfred is my Dad's name. This was the first time I found out that my Dad was coming in for an outpatient procedure!

But although the doctors and hospital knocked off most of the bill, I was left with about $20,000 to pay. Twenty thousand dollars is a lot, but it is only money. I had paid off over twice that amount after my wife's wreck, so although that was a lot of money, it did not crush me. I was an experienced hospital bill payer, and even though it seemed my world was coming apart, at least I hadn't lost a daughter this time! Money can always be replaced! Children are priceless and can never be replaced! There will always be a hole in me where Jennifer should have been. It wasn't money that was crushing me this time. What was crushing me was the divorce I didn't want and the prospect of losing my boys!

# Chapter 5

## Darkness and Dark Poems

My boys were now, after I lost my wife through divorce, everything! I was determined to not be a part-time Dad. I convinced my soon to be ex-wife that the boys would be better under joint custody. I never thought about it at the time, but why was it easy to convince her? She had never shown that she believed in the importance of a Dad or the father of the children. But I took it as a victory, one of the very few without the question. I would have them every other weekend with the reverse happening during the summers. Even though I lived four hundred miles away, I would, and did, keep the responsibility of being there for my sons!

It was then that I wrote the next poems:

# Questions that Haunt
## Steve (Moochie)

I cannot know the why
I can only live until I die
For I only know the questions
The questions that haunts my heart
Like what I feel now we're apart
The pain may someday pass
But it just might leave a lifeless heart


# Be Fair
## Moochie

Above all be fair
For everything you do
Will be either add to you
Or it will be subtracted from you


Then I fell into the darkness. Isn't the darkness of night always followed by the light of day, at that time I didn't believe it did!

# Nightmare
Steve (Moochie) Knowles

Nothing seems real
The nightmare only grows darker and darker still
Oh, God, please, give me light
So I can walk on this darkest of nights
For I stumble and fall
As my eyes can see nothing at all

# What Am I?
Steve (Moochie) Knowles

What am I?
Just a moment in time
A brief spark then cold ash

Who am I?
A forgotten soul
A tormented spirit lost

Why am I?
Is there a reason
A purpose great enough to justify
I do not know the answers
I only know the questions
And it's the questions that haunt me

# When It's Dark
Steve (Moochie) Knowles

When it's dark
And you can't see
Turn around
You just might find me

# A LONELY WALK
Moochie

Alone inside the corridors of my mind
I walk alone down this well-worn path
I walk in silence, making no sound
I walk alone just making my rounds
Who sees what does not happen
Who hears what is not spoken
Who knocks where no one calls

# Listen
## Moochie

When the world beats you down
And you call for help
But there is no one around
Do you listen with your ears?
For an answer that never comes
For there is no one to hear
So do you listen with your heart?
And risk it tearing you apart
But what would you do if you had no heart
To tear you apart

# When Love Goes
## Moochie

Feel for those who are in the battle to keep it
For they have to feel the pain of it when it goes
Feel for those who can never have it
For they will never feel the magic or the pain of love
So without love's magic there is also no pain
But instead there is nothing at all

# I Am Not
## Moochie

If I cannot be what I am
So I must be what I am not
And if I am what I am not
Then I must not exist
For I am not

# Some People
## Steve (Moochie) Knowles

Do things for others out of love
Do things for others and charge a fee
Get pleasure from seeing others happy
Get pleasure from seeing others in pain
Achieve success from working with others
Achieve success from using others
Have friendships for lasting companionship
Have acquaintances to be used and discarded
Give, not keeping track of any score
Only give to keep track of their score
The score to be used later for their own gain

# A New World
### Steve (Moochie) Knowles

As I enter this new world I have terrifying fears
All I know is I am here I'm not sure where here is
Do I know anyone here?
Is everyone here a loser?
How long do I stay here?
Do I ever leave here?
If I find a door do I open it?
Doors go both ways
If I see someone inviting
How do I trust my judgment?
Will I color everything to fit my wants?
Will I only see what I want to see?
Not wanting to be alone will I be too hasty?
Wanting to hold and be held
Will I be able to tell the actors from the real people?

# When No One Can Hear You Cry

Steve (Moochie) Knowles

When no one can hear you cry
When you are surrounded by people
Yet no one can see the pain
When everyone else is laughing
And you are crying
When everyone else is standing in sunlight
And you are hiding in the shadows
When the smiles you wear make
everyone think you are happy
While sadness weighs like an anchor around your neck
When you need help
And all you get is advice
When no one can hear you cry
You know it's time to leave
You know it's time to die

I am certain that many people go through this period after a divorce, and most of them believe, at the time, that they are alone in the depression of it. Some friends opened my eyes to this and convinced me I was in that darkness. But I was not alone in the darkness. They also reminded me that after the night comes the morning. If it helps just one other going through this despair to see the light at the end of the tunnel, then it is worth it!

# Chapter 6

# After the Darkness, Light from Friends

Since I could not go any farther down that path, I had to make a decision about my life. A classmate and his wife gave me a place to leave my boys during the day the first summer that I had the boys with me. Peggy Herndon noticed my problems taking care of my boys, not having any help. She decided to step up and offer some help. She told me that any time I had to leave them with her to just call and drop them off. She said she probably wouldn't even notice having a couple of extra mouths to feed! I didn't use it very often. Karol, my brother Bob's oldest daughter, offered to stay with my boys while I worked. But just knowing I had people willing to step up and help was a good feeling!

It had been a few years from the ripping apart of my marriage when my oldest boy John, thirteen, started getting into actual fist fights with his step-dad. I had told John that if he wanted to leave that situation and live with me, it would be okay with me. My ex-wife was furious. It became two warring camps as my ex-wife no longer wanted to discuss the situation or try a different arrangement. Not even on a temporary basis. John's next birthday would be his fourteenth, the age when he could choose where to live. Then my younger son, Marc, expressed his desire to stay with his older brother. The situation with John would be only a few months away. Adding the Marc situation turned the war into Armageddon!

Marc was only ten and was almost four years from being able to choose. I tried to get Marc to understand he would be leaving his mother at an age that I believed he needed her. Since my ex-wife and I were not on speaking terms, I could not discuss it with her. But he said what he really wanted was to be with his older brother, John. And since I could not find out anything from her about the situation in her house, I relented and told him okay.

My ex-wife had already hired her lawyer, so discussing the situation was impossible, even if she would agree to it. So I had to hire a lawyer to even talk to her! It was lawyer talking to lawyer time! My ex-wife would not consider anything different than her demands, so it became court time. The proceeding court battle didn't last very long. When the situation of having fights in my ex-wife's home came out, her lawyer quickly scrambled to get her cut. The offer was made that if I would pay all the court costs and both lawyers, the judge would grant me to be the main custodian of both boys. Not the best deal for me, but the boys would be living with me, and I guess that was what it was all about, so I agreed. The judge set up the payment of $800 a month and stressed that had to be paid each month or my ex-wife could sue and have me back in court! It's amazing that the care of my boys would be less than the need for money for the lawyers! No matter what, they had to be first in line.

It had taken us almost fourteen years to pay off the medical bills of her wreck. The wreck wasn't my fault, but the not being able to understand all insurance language was my fault. I thought all the big numbers were for both parties, but our side had only $3,000 major medical. Now I was having to also pay court and lawyer bills each month! All because of my belief that having a Dad in the home that cares about his kids is important!

I had accepted my financial state as it wasn't the important thing in my life. But I was having second thoughts about my decision not to sue the doctors who really messed up on my care. But that was too late. I was going to be back in the quagmire of bills from my stay in the hospital. And now I had the bills from my battle over my boys! It was very depressing, and it almost brought me to the point of wanting an exit from my life! But my boys now needed me more than ever! So I just kept battling; I knew of nothing else.

Just like Mike and Peggy Herndon, others stepped up. Mike and Betty Teter, Herb Shaffer, David and Dana Hansen, Dr. Richard, Steve and Maxie Steeby, Phil and Judy Wohlford, Richard and Cheryl Freeman, my four brothers and their wives all stepped up with help. I had many to fight off the sorrow and depression that was ME.

Tomorrow
Moochie

I do not know what comes with tomorrow
But should tomorrow never come
And today is all there is
Then I would like to spend my today
With friends like all of you

The 1990s continued with more stress than content-
ment, more trips to, and more stays in hospitals. On top of
the inherited problems with my heart, I also went through
a surgery to fix a hernia I had from work. My medical
problems just kept coming! After recovering from the hernia surgery, I ran head-on into another very serious issue.

One day I stopped at a hospital emergency room
because I was having trouble breathing. I thought I might
have pneumonia. I figured they would give me some drugs
and I would pay and be on my way. Nothing ever works
that easy for me. They admitted me as a patient and told
me what was wrong with me. They said I needed a new
heart, and the waiting list was long and I didn't have that
much time left. So they put me in a room and told me that
they would make my last days as comfortable and painless
as possible! I appreciated their concern, and for the ump-
teenth time, I was ready to accept my fate.

David Hansen came to visit me in the hospital, and I
told him what the doctors had said. David had a sugges-
tion, "How about getting a second opinion, Mooch?" So
he called Dr. Richard Steckley who said, "Get him ready,

I'm sending an ambulance over to get him." So I was transferred to a different hospital that quickly! Dr. Richard told David after checking things, "He doesn't need a new heart; he needs a new heart valve!"

I wonder how many people die because they don't have a Dr. Richard in their corner! So with Dr. Richard in charge of my heart care, my medical problems took a turn from "poor" to "great!" His team first did an open heart surgery to install a "pig" valve. A "pig" valve can last as long as ten years. But because of an infection in my teeth, this one lasted only eight years.

After this last escapade and my history of medical horror stories, I asked Dr. Richard, my cardiologist, to be my "everything" doctor. I told him to just get me to our fiftieth high school reunion in 2017, and I would be happy. Yes, "our," as Dr. Richard and I go back a long way, grade school, high school! In fact, my first sleepover was at Richard's house. I was six or seven, and his house was the first house I had ever been in that had air conditioning! I had never slept in air conditioning before, and boy did I get sick! Richard's Mom was the nicest Mom on the face of the earth at that time! I wasn't at my best, throwing up and all. But with her help I made it through!

Because of the infection with my teeth, I had a mechanical heart valve put in with more open heart surgery by Dr. Richard's team. But I also had my teeth pulled! But I think they used the same cut lines on the heart surgery, so the scar on my chest stayed the same! At least I had health insurance this time!

I still have health problems, but I think I have the best health care in the world now! About fifteen years ago, Dr.

Richard set up an appointment with a diabetes doctor, Dr. Challans. Something had showed up on my blood test! I had diabetes, wonderful, just what I was missing on my medical "bucket list!" After a while of using injections to treat my blood sugar, I started learning how I could control my diabetes with my diet. I no longer need insulin.

About nine years ago, something once again showed up on a blood sample that raised a red flag. Dr. Richard sent me to an urologist, Dr. Zakharia, to get it checked out. It turned out that this time I did have cancer, prostate cancer! Hey bucket list, got room for one more? But with some gold chips inserted "you know where" and a "Cyber Knife" machine, the cancer was defeated, at least at that time!

In 2012, I had to go through the ordeal explained in the short story titled "The Empty Chair." Where my right leg started turning almost black, and the group of friends after one of our poker games took a look at my blackening leg and said, "Moochie, they cut things that look like that off!" Yes, it was David again, and he was right, AGAIN! Bucket list, table for one? So I had to have my right leg amputated below the knee.

The amputation was predicted by Dr. Richard. He said that with all the procedures that he had done, I would probably start losing "parts" the next time! He coordinated the amputation with his team and the doctor, Dr. Anthony Pollock, who did the amputation. I guess that was the "parts" that Dr. Richard predicted. My health ordeals seemed to be endless.

A few years later I was told my PSA blood level showed indications of the prostate cancer returning. I think I probably received the cancer speech a little differently than most patients do. If it is the third time you hear it, it loses a lot of its impact! To keep the cancer in check during my six months between my doctor appointments with the urologist was shots . . . Why is it always SHOTS? Shots hurt, and for days after they still hurt! . . . I receive one shot for the cancer and another for the osteoporosis that is caused by the cancer shot. Hey, bucket list, got room? As Dick Clark used to say on his weekly show, *American Bandstand*, which was about the current hits (at that time it was great "rock and roll" songs), "And the hits just keep on coming!"

Yes, things have not always been "hunky-dory" in other ways either, as I can still mess up with no help from anyone. A couple of years ago, I had what I thought was a "minor" fall. I started having blood in my urine and had a real fun time with my hospital stay during that! Things like having a nurse try to insert a catheter that was too long for the job! SO YOU WANT TO FEEL PAIN, try that! So it still isn't fun and games, but I'll let everybody know if I survive! On second thought I'll have somebody else do that if I don't survive! Does this go on the bucket list?

I did make it to my fiftieth high school reunion, so Dr. Richard had performed his mass of miracles. But I did have an experience there that exposed a chink in my armor. During our dinner, Dr. Richard asked me what I wanted to eat as I was in my wheelchair. I was recovering from all the walking I did during the Bar-B-Q at Dr. Richard's house the night before. I wasn't thinking real clearly and ordered something that would have to be cut up to eat. It hit me as I watched Dr. Richard bring it to our table that it would take a knife in one hand and a fork in the other. That would have been easy, but I had only one hand that worked, not two!

Now I had to find a way to pull this off as I had never told Dr. Richard about my left hand being pretty much worthless. I tried to act like nothing was wrong, but the more I tried to hide it . . . the worse my problem became . . . until it became obvious to everyone at our table, including Dr. Richard's wife! As every time I dropped one of my utensils, Dr. Richard would get up and get me another. It was getting almost comedic, but nobody was laughing! Except maybe Dr. Richard, as he could always keep a straight face while playing a joke. He was not involved in the cause of this comedy. He didn't even have to be involved I was making a fool of myself without any outside help! I finally just pushed my plate away and gave up.

The following Monday I found the courage to admit my lies and begged him to forgive me. He answered with his question for me of "what were the symptoms?" I gave them and he set up the appointment to get my nerves in my hand and arm checked out. No condemnation for my not being honest, just let's find out what the problem is! That turned out to be my next surgery. The appointment showed I had pinched nerves and carpel tunnel in my left hand and left arm. So Dr. Chan entered my list of doctors. In fact my bucket list is beginning to look like a telephone directory of great doctors! The surgery went well, and I was out the same day! I just had to learn and DO some exercises with my left hand. They told me the damage could not be fixed (returned to normal). But I could learn to adapt with a serious exercise schedule and a lot of determination to stick to it.

Even though I tried to hide my problem and basically lied to him, Dr. Richard is still trying to now get me to our fifty-fifth high school reunion. Dr. Richard doesn't know how to quit! It's kind of funny that I tried to not use my connection with Dr. Richard in entering the quagmire that was my medical history, but when he jumped in, he became the reason I'm still here! Most people would say that they only knew one or maybe two friends that were true friends to all their high school friends. I have been lucky enough to have many! Dr. Richard is one of the best ones!

My oldest son, John, graduated from our high school, Goddard High, in 1995. He marvels at how close our class has been and how close we are today. John said he had maybe two still close friends out of the hundreds that were in his class. If we are the anomaly, then we should point out that it takes a lot of work to keep class members close. I've been told it's like herding cats! But it is a journey of love, as these class members and friends are the ones who we not only grew up with but did everything with; we played, we laughed, and we cried with all of them. By the way, having reunions on a five-year plan helps keep the class closer together as it is all about personal contact. Whoever "gets stuck (gets the honor)" of contacting everyone acts out of the love that all of us feel about each other.

I think it is sad how people seem to have forgotten the intimacy of face to face talking, of taking the time to make a phone call, or writing a letter. It's sad to see a world moving away from the intimate friendships that made my life worth living. My journey of life, which began long ago, evolved into something totally different from I see surrounding all of the people of today. If your story has friendships like mine, you know the blessings they bring. If you don't have good friends, it's not too late. As long as there is breath in you, you can reach out and be the catalyst. Pick up the phone . . .

I hope you have enjoyed this look of all the times of Steve (me) and Moochie (also me) and all the kids, all the teenagers, and all the people we and they did become and have joined me and Moochie (also me) in the adventures of all of us! Let's just hope the "statute of limitations" has expired!

Steve was born in Dodge City, Kansas. The 1940s were ending, and the 1950s were getting ready to start. In 1956, the Knowles family moved into the town of Goddard, Kansas. It was in Goddard that Moochie was born, or actually became the six-and-a-half-year-old Steve's nickname, alias, or alter ego. After Moochie's many adventures, Steve returned to the town he loved as a child, Goddard. Nowadays he spends his time retelling those travels and tales to entertain his grandchildren. Always hoping they too will have stories of their own to tell and entertain their grandchildren.

Now Steve's first love was baseball, and he coached youth baseball for over twenty-five years. He also started "Operation Home Run, Kansas." Operation Home Run was started because two soldiers in Kuwait wanted to have something to do while waiting for orders. A phone call came from Marc Knowles to his Dad with a request for a couple baseball gloves and a baseball. After those things arrived in Kuwait, Marc phoned again with this request, "Dad, you do know that there are 150,000 of us over here. Can you send more?" Operation Home Run started the next day. The only request Steve made was that he would want the baseball equipment to stay there in Iraq for the Iraqi kids! That's my Dad, always believing kids playing baseball could change the world!

—John Knowles, the other brother

CPSIA information can be obtained
at www.ICGtesting.com
Printed in the USA
LVHW111449211118
597913LV00001B/83/P